Loading 1,000-pounders into the bomb bay of a 49 Squadron Avro Lincoln B.2 at Eastleigh, Nairobi, Kenya. The unit had deployed to Eastleigh on November 11, 1953 from Wittering as the state of emergency against rebels from the Kenya Land Freedom Party, known as the 'Mau Mau', grew in intensity. British-based Lincoln units rotated out to Kenya until July 1955 when 21 Squadron returned to the UK by which time the Mau Mau had been defeated.

# CONTENTS

6    PER ARDUA AD ASTRA
8    DE HAVILLAND AMIENS
10   DE HAVILLAND DH.9A
12   VICKERS VIMY
14   AVRO ALDERSHOT
16   VICKERS VIRGINIA
18   FAIREY FAWN, FOX, GORDON
20   HANDLEY PAGE HYDERABAD AND HINAIDI
22   HAWKER HORSLEY
24   BOULTON AND PAUL SIDESTRAND AND
     OVERSTRAND
26   HAWKER HART AND HIND
28   VICKERS VILDEBEEST
30   HANDLEY PAGE HEYFORD
32   FAIREY HENDON
34   ARMSTRONG WHITWORTH WHITLEY
36   BRISTOL BLENHEIM
38   FAIREY BATTLE
40   VICKERS WELLESLEY
42   HANDLEY PAGE HAMPDEN AND HEREFORD
44   VICKERS WELLINGTON
46   BRISTOL BEAUFORT
48   AVRO MANCHESTER
50   SHORT STIRLING

52   HANDLEY PAGE HALIFAX
54   MARTIN MARYLAND AND BALTIMORE
56   AVRO LANCASTER
58   BOEING FORTRESS
60   CONSOLIDATED LIBERATOR
62   DE HAVILLAND MOSQUITO
64   DOUGLAS BOSTON
66   VULTEE VENGEANCE
68   LOCKHEED VENTURA
70   MARTIN MARAUDER
72   NORTH AMERICAN MITCHELL
76   AVRO LINCOLN
78   BRISTOL BLENHEIM
80   BOEING WASHINGTON
82   ENGLISH ELECTRIC CANBERRA
84   VICKERS VALIANT
86   AVRO VULCAN
88   HANDLEY PAGE VICTOR
90   HAWKER SIDDELEY BUCCANEER
92   PANAVIA TORNADO
94   BRITISH AEROSPACE/McDONNELL
     DOUGLAS HARRIER
96   LOCKHEED MARTIN LIGHTNING II

Edited by: **Ken Ellis**
With many thanks to: **Chris Gilson**
and **Steve Beebee** at *FlyPast*;
**Ajay Srivastava** at the RAF Museum;
**Andy Thomas** and **Sean Feast**
Contributing writers: **Steve Appleby,
Daniel Ford, Jonathan Garroway, Josh
Lyman, Bob Uppendaun** and **M L Wynche**
Group Editor: **Nigel Price**

Archive images: All **Key Collection** unless
noted
Artwork: **Andy Hay** - www.flyingart.co.uk
and in memory of **Pete West**

Art Editor: **Mike Carr**
Chief Designer: **Steve Donovan**

Production Editor: **Sue Blunt**
Deputy Production Editor: **Carol Randall**
Production Manager: **Janet Watkins**

Advertisement Manager: **Alison Sanders**
Advertising Production: **Debi McGowan**
Group Advertisement Manager:
**Brodie Baxter**

Marketing Executive: **Shaun Binnington**
Marketing Manager: **Martin Steele**

Commercial Director: **Ann Saundry**
Managing Director and Publisher:
**Adrian Cox**
Executive Chairman: **Richard Cox**

**Contacts**
Key Publishing Ltd, PO Box 100, Stamford,
Lincs, PE9 1XQ
Tel 01780 755131
Email flypast@keypublishing.com
www.keypublishing.com

Distribution: **Seymour Distribution Ltd,
2 Poultry Avenue, London EC1A 9PT**.
Tel **020 74294000**
Printed by: **Warners (Midland) plc,
The Maltings, Bourne, Lincs, PE10 9PH**

Published by: **Key
Publishing Ltd** - see above
**Printed in England**

**Front Cover:**
*Front Cover: Since
November 1973 Avro
Lancaster I PA474
has been a member
of the Battle of
Britain Memorial
Flight passing on
the unit's message
of 'Lest We Forget'
wherever it goes.
During that time its
paint schemes have
paid tribute to the
men and squadrons
of Bomber Command.
At present it wears
the markings of
460 Squadron Royal
Australian Air Force to
port and 50 Squadron
to starboard.*
JOHN DIBBS - PLANE
PICTURE COMPANY

**Inset:**
**Inset:** *During trials
in the USA an RAF
Lockheed Martin
F-35B carrying out
the retractable
in-flight refuelling
probe.*
COURTESY AND
COPYRIGHT LOCKHEED
MARTIN

**This page:**
*A trio of de Havilland
Mosquito B.35s of 139
Squadron ready for
take-off at their base,
Hemswell, in May
1950. Note that VP194
in the centre still has
black undersides;
whereas the overall
'silver' of VP185 and
TK620 flanking it
represent the final
colour scheme of
Bomber Command
Mosquitos. Beginning
with Mosquito IVs in
September 1942, the
unit stayed faithful
to the DH twin until
it traded in its B.35s
for English Electric
Canberra B.2s in 1953.*

## PER ARDUA
# AD ASTRA
## 1918 TO 2018

**Above**
*The Royal Air Force badge was approved by the Air Council on August 1, 1918: the original differing only slightly from today's version.*

**Right**
*De Havilland DH.4 A7995 parked out at its birthplace, the Aircraft Manufacturing Company's factory and airfield at Hendon in 1917. Today, Hendon is the headquarters of the RAF Museum and where the 'RAF First 100 Years' exhibition will be launched in the summer of 2018.*

When the Royal Air Force was established on April 1, 1918 there were pundits who doubted it would outlast the Great War and then the 'upstart' would be put back in its place. World events were to prove that the RAF was not a short-lived need but a fundamental requirement of modern defence.

Throughout its ten decades, the RAF has been frequently tested, but seldom found lacking. Its Latin motto, 'Per Ardua ad Astra', best translated as 'Through Adversity to the Stars', sums up its incredible achievements.

Royal ascent was granted to an Act of Parliament establishing the RAF and the Air Council on November 29, 1917. Prior to that there had been two air arms, with over-lapping operations, the Royal Flying Corps (RFC) and the Royal Naval Air Service (RNAS), each competing for resources and personnel. The RFC, established on March 13, 1912, had a Military Wing and a Naval Wing but from July 1914 the naval element became self-contained as the RNAS. The Air Force Constitution Act provided for amalgamation of the RFC and the RNAS and set the date for this to come into full force – April 1, 1918.

The Armistice that came into effect on the eleventh hour of the eleventh month in 1918 brought the horrific 'war to end all wars' to a close. Only 21 years later the world was again at war; this time a conflict in which aviation was to play a vital – not merely supportive – role.

The peace of 1945 proved to be transitory as a new clash developed; the so-called Cold War that lasted all the way to the dissolution of the Soviet Union in 1991. Beyond that the planet has been littered with armed dissent: global terrorist movements, brutal civil wars and the birth of another new buzzword – cyber warfare.

Countless words and images will be published during the RAF's centenary celebrations and deciding how to present a *FlyPast* 'special' that paid tribute in an original manner took some pondering. The team settled on telling the story of the RAF through its bombers and fighters in *two* publications. (If you missed the magazine devoted to the fighters you can still secure a copy. Details of how to order it appear elsewhere in this volume.)

### LINKED BY HERITAGE
Our romp through the RAF's bomber types starts with the de Havilland Amiens of 1918 and concludes with the Lockheed Martin Lightning II which will enter full squadron service at Marham this year. References vary about the extent of the US-designed warplane's payload, but 'formidable' would sum it up. Within its weapons bays and on its wing pylons it can likely carry *twice* the all-up weight of its de Havilland forebear of a century before.

Despite this yawning gulf of performance and statistics, both the Amiens and the F-35B are linked by more than their heritage: deterrence was and is their business. It is as well to remember that in 1918 the Amiens was not a slow, vulnerable 'stick and string' biplane, it was a state-of-the-art weapon wielded by a world power.

These pages show that in

F.5417.

5417 17

September 1939 the RAF still had biplane bombers on charge, although they were carrying out secondary tasks. World threats in the 1920s were 'low tech' but by the 1930s the pace of development had to quicken to meet a changing world.

Nineteen years separated the first flight of two Handley Page products, the O/400 of 1917 and the Hampden, and the difference in layout, construction and capability was vast. The prototype Avro Lancaster first took to the skies in 1941 – eleven years later the same company had flown the delta-winged, nuclear-capable Vulcan. Technology has continued to enhance the shape and scope of the RAF's aircraft.

## END OF AN ERA?

Since 2007 the RAF has had a new form of 'bomber' in its arsenal. This type is not included in depth within this magazine because, for the first time, the RAF has a frontline aircraft that does not have a cockpit.

Operating from Afghanistan but piloted from Creech Air Force Base in Nevada, USA, in May 2008 the RAF began to drop precision-guided weapons from its General Atomics MQ-9A Reapers. In British parlance these machines are called RPAS – remotely piloted air systems. They point to the future, but Reapers have severe limitations, they can only function in uncontested airspace.

The words 'bomber' and 'fighter' have become more and more difficult to define. With the advent of the Lightning II these labels are so blurred that a new name is called for. The RAF describes the F-35B as a "multi-role supersonic stealth aircraft that will provide the UK with a hugely capable and flexible weapons and sensor platform".

Looking *beyond* the F-35 and the Eurofighter Typhoon the design teams at BAE Systems are busy testing their ideas for combat aircraft for the 2030s. While heralding a new era during the RAF's centenary celebrations

it might well be that Marham's Lightning IIs mark the twilight of the piloted warplane.

## TURKEYS AND TRIUMPHS

Inside this publication the reader will find every manned frontline bomber type that the RAF has operated in its 100 years. Already we can 'hear' the cries of anguish: "Only two pages on the Lancaster?" With limited space, to make sure that *all* the RAF's fighters get a mention, the most well-known have been slimmed down.

In the pages that follow are a few turkeys, but most of the RAF's bombers have been triumphs. The emphasis is less about derring-do; seasoned *FlyPast* readers will already be well versed in the valour and exploits of RAF personnel.

Here, the intention is to be concerned with where the subject fits in the RAF's centenary and its heritage, or even in the context of world aviation history. The hope is that the reader will find more than a few "I never knew that" moments as we pay tribute to the finest air force in the world. ◉

**Above**
*Handley Page O/400 F5417 was built at National Aircraft Factory 1 at Waddon, Surrey, in 1918. Underneath the centre section is a 1,650lb bomb.*
PETE WEST

**Below**
*BAE Systems Taranis ZZ250 during test flying in Australia in 2014. Taranis, named after the Celtic god of thunder, is an unmanned combat air system demonstrator and part of a comprehensive series of trials that BAE Systems has been conducting towards the RAF's next generation of warplanes.*
COURTESY AND COPYRIGHT BAE SYSTEMS

# DE HAVILLAND
# AMIENS

## 1918 TO 1923

**Top right and above**
*The second prototype DH.10, C8659, at a muddy Hendon in the spring of 1918. It was powered by a pair of tractor 36 0hp Rolls-Royce Eagles and first flew on April 20.*
BOTH PETER GREEN COLLECTION

### DE HAVILLAND AMIENS III

| | |
|---|---|
| **Type:** | Four-seat day bomber |
| **First flight:** | March 4, 1918, entered service November 1918 |
| **Powerplant:** | One 400hp (298kW) Packard Liberty 12 V12 |
| **Dimensions:** | Span 65ft 6in (19.96m), Length 39ft 7½in (12.07m) |
| **Weights:** | Empty 5,585lb (2,533kg), All-up 9,000lb (4,082kg) |
| **Max speed:** | 112mph (180km/h) at 10,000ft (3,048m) |
| **Range:** | Endurance 6 hours |
| **Armament:** | One machine gun in nose and dorsal positions. Up to 900lb (408kg) of bombs |
| **Replaced:** | De Havilland DH.9s from late 1918 |
| **Taken on charge:** | About 260 |
| **Replaced by:** | De Havilland DH.9As and Vickers Vimys by 1923 |

Officially named Amiens, the de Havilland biplane bomber was referred to almost exclusively by its designation, DH.10. Geoffrey de Havilland was employed as designer and test pilot for George Holt Thomas's The Aircraft Manufacturing Company – widely shortened to Airco – from May 1914. During this time, all of Geoffrey's creations carried his initials.

By 1920, Airco had reached the DH.18 and the end of the economic road, closing its Hendon factory that year. Geoffrey de Havilland went on to form his own company in his own name.

As a response to the bombing of Britain by Imperial German forces with Zeppelin airships in January 1915, larger aircraft capable of taking the fight to German territory were ordered by the Air Ministry. Geoffrey de Havilland responded with the twin-engined DH.10, which he took for its maiden flight on March 4, 1918. This prototype was powered by a pair of pusher BHP engines of 240hp (179kW).

Nineteen days after the formation of the Royal Air Force, the second DH.10 was air tested. This one was fitted with tractor powerplants, a pair of 360hp Rolls-Royce Eagles, and its performance was very promising.

On May 13 the formation of the Independent Air Force was announced with the main aim of hitting targets in Germany and Major General Sir Hugh Trenchard took command on June 6. There were great hopes that this force would provide the hammer blow that would bring Germany to surrender.

A surge in bomber orders resulted and 1,300 DH.10s were requested from Airco. To meet this huge demand, sub-contracts with five other manufacturers were placed. Production versions of the Amiens were designated Mk.III and fitted with American-made Packard Liberty V12s.

The first unit to operate the type was 104 Squadron at Azelot, south of Nancy, taking delivery in the early days of November 1918. Part of the Independent Air Force, 104 took part in a large raid on aerodromes in German-held northern France on November 10. Captain Ewart John Garland flew F1867 of 104 Squadron to attack Sarrebourg, to the east of Nancy.

The following day, at 11 o'clock the armistice came into force and the DH.10's contribution to the war remained solitary. As with many other types, contracts for Amiens were slashed and only about 260 were completed.

### FIGHTING WARLORDS

A small number of DH.10s soldiered on into 1923 with two units claiming the honour of being the last to fly the big biplane. In Egypt, 216 Squadron had flown DH.10s since December 1919. Amiens were used to fly personnel

and air mail from Cairo to Baghdad, Iraq. Navigation across the featureless desert was facilitated by a simple aid, 'pointers' in the sand made from a mixture of thick oil and hessian.

Retirement began in the summer of 1922, but it was April the following year before the last example was withdrawn at Heliopolis in favour of Vickers Vimys.

Captain Garland's sortie of November 10, 1918 turned out not to be the only time that the Amiens dropped bombs in anger. On April 1, 1920 at Lahore in India, 60 Squadron was re-formed and moved to Risalpur, between Islamabad and Kabul.

Equipped with never more than six DH.10s, during November 1920 the squadron was involved in almost daily punitive raids against Afghan warlords in what the British 'Raj' referred to as the North West Frontier. That area flared up again in 1922 and, during the same year, the unit was also in combat with Waziristani tribesmen to the south.

By February 1923 there was just a pair of airworthy DH.10s with 60 Squadron. In April the much more flexible and durable DH.9A took over from the lumbering Amiens. 'Nine Acks' – see page 10 – served 60 Squadron, quelling dissident warriors until 1930. ◎

# AVIATION SPECIALS

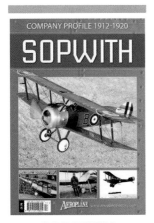

### SOPWITH
Looks at all the types produced by this prolific manufacturer.

**£6.99** inc FREE P&P*

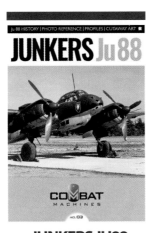

### JUNKERS JU88
Combat Machines Volume 3 explores the German Luftwaffe's famous bomber, the Ju 88, in all its variants.

**£7.99** inc FREE P&P*

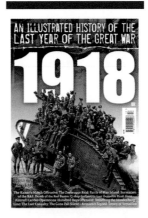

### 1918: AN ILLUSTRATED HISTORY
This is the story of the Great War's final year.

**£6.99** inc FREE P&P*

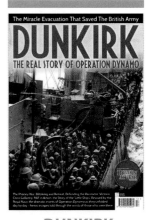

### DUNKIRK
The story of the great evacuation is told, day-by-day.

**£6.99** inc FREE P&P*

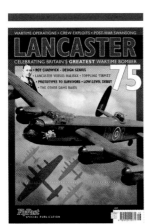

### LANCASTER 75
Pays tribute to all who built, maintained and flew Lancasters, past and present.

**£5.99** inc FREE P&P*

### RAF ANNUAL REVIEW
132-page special providing behind the scenes insight into the aircraft, equipment, people and operations of one of the world's premier air forces.

**£6.99** inc FREE P&P*

### FIGHTERS OF THE RAF CENTENARY
A unique tribute to the fighters that have defended Britain and fought in conflicts across the world since 1918.

**£5.99** inc FREE P&P*

### BRITISH PHANTOMS
It is hard to believe that 25 years have passed since the RAF retired its 'Phinal Phantom', in October 1992.

**£5.99** inc FREE P&P*

# AVIATION SPECIALS

**ESSENTIAL** reading from the teams behind your **FAVOURITE** magazines

## HOW TO ORDER

 **OR**

**PHONE**
UK: 01780 480404
ROW: (+44)1780 480404

**FREE Aviation Specials App**

Simply download to purchase digital versions of your favourite aviation specials in one handy place! Once you have the app, you will be able to download new, out of print or archive specials for less than the cover price!

IN APP ISSUES **£3.99**

*Prices correct at time of going to press. Free 2nd class P&P on all UK & BFPO orders.
Overseas charges apply. Postage charges vary depending on total order value.

# DE HAVILLAND
# DH.9A
## 1918 TO 1931

**Right**
*Built by Airco in 1919, DH.9A E8673 was converted into a dual-control trainer in the early 1920s. By 1923 it was serving 27 Squadron – as illustrated – from Risalpur, India. This machine was finally retired in 1930.* KEC

One of the most significant British aircraft of the Great War was the de Havilland DH.4 two-place light bomber which became operational in January 1917. It was fast and manoeuvrable and the concept inspired the DH.4's designer, Geoffrey de Havilland, to initiate the Mosquito 23 years later.

In July 1917 a much-improved version was flown, the DH.9 which was fitted with a 230hp (171kW) Siddeley Puma in its production form. This turned out to be the right airframe but the wrong engine. The Puma was dogged by troubles, so much so that the DH.4 was returned to production to meet the shortfall.

De Havilland turned to the well-proven Rolls-Royce Eagle and, later, the American-produced Packard Liberty 12 to replace the Puma. The result was the exceptionally reliable, adaptable and long-lived DH.9A. Based on early telegraphy phonetics the new type was known as the 'Nine Ack'.

Large-scale manufacture of the new type was entrusted to Westland and the prototype appeared in February 1918. Rushed into production, DH.9As were first issued to 110 Squadron in France on the last day of August 1918. Raids on targets in southern Germany, from 17,000ft (5,200m), began immediately and to good effect.

The Nine Ack became a trusted workhorse for post-war RAF

bomber units in Britain and it was widely used by the Auxiliary Air Force squadrons from their inception in 1925. It was in the Middle East and India where DH.9As gained a reputation for durability.

Westland devised many improvements and the final examples featured metal-framed wings. The last DH.9A came off the production line in May 1927. The stock of airframe spares for the Nine Ack was such that when Westland pitched for the type's replacement the resulting design, the Wapiti general purpose biplane, used many DH.9A components.

## DE HAVILLAND DH.9A

| | |
|---|---|
| **Type:** | Two-seat day bomber / general purpose |
| **First flight:** | February 1918, entered service June 1918 |
| **Powerplant:** | One 400hp (298kW) Packard Liberty 12A V12 |
| **Dimensions:** | Span 46ft 0in (14.0m), Length 30ft 0in (9.1m) |
| **Weights:** | Empty 2,695lb (1,222kg), All-up 4,645lb (2,106kg) |
| **Max speed:** | 114mph (183km/h) at 10,000ft (3,048m) |
| **Range:** | Endurance 5 hours, 45 minutes |
| **Armament:** | One 0.303in machine gun firing through propeller arc, another in rear position. Up to 450lb (204kg) of bombs |
| **Replaced:** | DH.4s and DH.9s from 1918 |
| **Taken on charge:** | 2,215, including some rebuilt airframes in the 190s. Sub-contracts to F W Berwick of London, Mann Egerton of Norwich, Vulcan Motor of Southport, Westland, Whitehead Aircraft of Richmond |
| **Replaced by:** | Fairey Fawn from 1924, Westland Wapiti from 1931 |

## WHITES VERSUS REDS
Long before the term 'Cold War' was even dreamed of, Britain clashed with Soviet forces during an unfortunate campaign from 1918 to 1920. A revolution in March 1917 brought about the abdication of Czar Nicholas II and the instigation of a republic. In November Bolshevik forces led by Vladimir Lenin and Leon Trotsky seized the initiative, beginning the imposition of a communist state which was eventually achieved after five years of bloody civil war.

Britain was one of several nations determined to intervene and an expeditionary force was deployed

**Left**
*Westland-built 'Nine Ack' H3510 of 8 Squadron based at Hinaidi, Iraq, with the gunner training his Lewis gun on the terrain below. This machine served 8 Squadron from early 1925 until 1926. Note the upper wing long-range tank, the spare wheel housed between the main undercarriage, night-landing flares under the outer wings and an empty stores 'cage' under the centre section.* KEC

**Below**
*Siddeley Puma-powered DH.9 D5694 in typical 1918 colours. This machine was built by London-based furniture manufacturer Waring and Gillow.* © ANDY HAY WWW. flyingart.co.uk

to Murmansk in Arctic northwest Russia on August 2, 1918. The air element, including DH.9As, set up at Bereznik, southeast of Archangel. The Bolsheviks were labelled by the world's press as 'Reds' and the counter-revolutionary forces became the 'Whites'.

Communications with White forces were chaotic, the freezing conditions neutered most operations and the supply chain – by sea around Scandinavia – was tortuously long. It was no surprise when British forces were instructed to withdraw in August 1919.

The Murmansk adventure was not the only British incursion into the Russian Civil War. Another expeditionary force landed on the northern shores of the Black Sea, at Batum in Georgia on January 3,

1919. Equipped with DH.9s and Nine Acks, 221 Squadron deployed eastwards – by train – to Petrovsk on the Caspian Sea. From there 221 was engaged in sporadic sorties until it was disbanded in September 1919.

By May 1919 the mixed bag of DH.9s and Sopwith Camels of 47 Squadron was based at Ekaterinodar on the Black Sea. The unit was swollen by DH.9As from the former 221 Squadron in October. During that month, it was decided that politically it was wrong to have operational RAF units within Russia and 47 was renamed as 'A' Squadron of the British Training Mission. The instructional intent not withstanding, this unit carried out its last bombing raid on suspected Soviet cavalry on March 28, 1930.

To return to the fortunes of 221

Squadron, in *RAF Operations 1918 to 1938* (Kimber, 1988) Chaz Bowyer quoted the diary of armourer D B Knock for mid-February 1919. "Two Nine Acks go on reconnaissance north, each with two 65- and two 230-pounders. South of Astrakhan they spot a parade of cavalry with red pennons flying. Drop the 'pills' [bombs] and get photos. Return and develop [the pictures] in glee showing much carnage. One up against the Reds."

Knock recorded that three days later the unit had a visit: "Cossack officer of high rank arrives with interpreter. Story gets around. That was no Red cavalry bombed, but the side we are supposed to be assisting. Our planes had decimated a squadron of White cavalry... Thought that Cossack looked furious. No wonder!" ◉

"Our planes had decimated a squadron of White cavalry... Thought that Cossack looked furious. No wonder!"

# VICKERS
# VIMY
## 1919 TO 1933

A long with the Handley Page O/400 and the de Havilland Amiens, the Vickers Vimy was designed as a bomber capable of striking at the cities of Imperial Germany. These aircraft were generically called 'Berlin Bombers' in the British press. The prototype Vimy first flew at Brooklands on November 30, 1917 and several engine alternatives were tried before the Rolls-Royce Eagle was chosen for the definitive Mk.IV.

Orders for 1,500 were placed, but events overtook the bomber. A single example was delivered to France in late October 1918, but it was not used in anger. With the Armistice, contracts were torn up and only about 200 Vimys were accepted for service. In 1919 Vickers was commissioned to build another 30 Mk.IVs and refurbish earlier examples.

The Vimy became world famous when John Alcock and Arthur Whitten Brown flew a Vickers-owned, specially modified, example non-stop across the Atlantic over June 14-15, 1919. The epic flight covered 1,890 miles (3,041km) in 15hrs 57mins at an average speed of 118.5mph (190km/h) from St John's, Newfoundland, to Clifden, Ireland. On December 15, 1919 the transatlantic Vimy was handed over to the Science Museum in London, where it still takes pride of place.

The first operational RAF unit to adopt the Vimy was 58 Squadron at Heliopolis, Egypt, in July 1919, replacing a handful of O/400s. This unit was re-numbered as 70 Squadron and it decamped, along with its Vimys, to Iraq in February 1920.

In Egypt, 216 Squadron took delivery of Vimy IVs in June 1922, replacing its ageing DH Amiens. The unit was engaged in the Cairo to Baghdad mail run and Vimys served in this role until January 1926.

## 'STRATEGIC' THOUGHTS

The Versailles Treaty of 1919 and in the following year the creation of a forum to resolve international crises, the League of Nations, gave hope that a new world order had been established. This and Britain's poor financial circumstances allowed the RAF of the 1920s to concentrate its assets on colonial matters, in the Middle East and in India where 'aerial policing' became the norm.

The RAF's Independent Air Force had shown a flash of potential in the final months of the Great War. The notion of 'strategic' bombers was still in its infancy and, especially for Britain, the task of deterrence remained firmly vested in the Royal Navy.

By January 1920 the small force of O/400 and V/1500 'heavies' had been withdrawn and the RAF's home-based long-range striking force was reduced to just 'D' Flight of 100 Squadron at Spitalgate, which flew Vimys alongside the rest of the unit's DH.9As.

It was June 1923 before there was a dedicated Vimy unit, 7 Squadron at Bircham Newton. It was quickly followed by 9 Squadron at

> "By January 1920 ...the RAF's home-based long-range striking force was reduced to just 100 Squadron at Spitalgate, which flew Vimys alongside the rest of the unit's DH.9As."

F9157

Manston, 58 at Worthy Down and 99, also based at Bircham Newton.

With a range of around 900 miles (1,448km) the Vimy could fly from Kent or Norfolk, hit Berlin and return to base – with favourable winds, a flight time of about 8hrs. But in the 1920s the German capital was not envisaged as a target, nor was any western European city.

Training regimes for the RAF's British-based Vimys included the capability to hit warships – surface vessels and submarines – and

## VICKERS VIMY IV

| | |
|---|---|
| Type: | Three-seat heavy bomber |
| First flight: | November 30, 1917, entered service July 1918 |
| Powerplant: | Two 360hp (368kW) Rolls-Royce Eagle VIII V12 |
| Dimensions: | Span 68ft 1in (20.7m), Length 43ft 6½in (13.25m) |
| Weights: | Empty 7,100lb (3,220kg), All-up 12,500lb (5,670kg) |
| Max speed: | 100mph (160km/h) at 6,500ft (1,981m) |
| Range: | About 900 miles (1,448km) |
| Armament: | One machine gun in nose position, twin machine gun in dorsal position. Up to 2,500lb (1,134kg) of bombs |
| Replaced: | Handley Page O/400 from 1919 |
| Taken on charge: | circa 250 |
| Replaced by: | Vickers Virginia from 1924 |

maintaining a readiness to deploy to 'hot spots' as they developed in the colonies.

From 1924 Vimys gave way to Vickers Virginias, which were to hold the line well into the 1930s. Retired Vimys took up crew training and trials roles, the last of the breed being withdrawn in 1933. ◉

**Above**
*Shown inside the Grahame-White Factory display hall at Hendon, the RAF Museum's Vimy is presently kept at the Stafford storage facility. Built as a faithful replica by the Vintage Aircraft and Flying Association and first flew at Brooklands on June 6, 1969. It carries the name 'Triple First' on the nose to denote the first Atlantic, Australia and South Africa flights undertaken by Vimys, 1919-1920. KEN ELLIS*

**Left**
*Vimy IV H657 flying over Cairo in mid-1926. It started off as Mk.III F2920 with Fiat A-12 engines built at the Royal Aircraft Establishment at Farnborough in mid-1918. (The Royal Aircraft Factory was renamed as the RAE on April, 1, 1918.) Rebuilt as a Mk.IV by Vickers at Brooklands in the early 1920s, it entered service with 216 Squadron at Heliopolis, Egypt, in the spring of 1925. KEC*

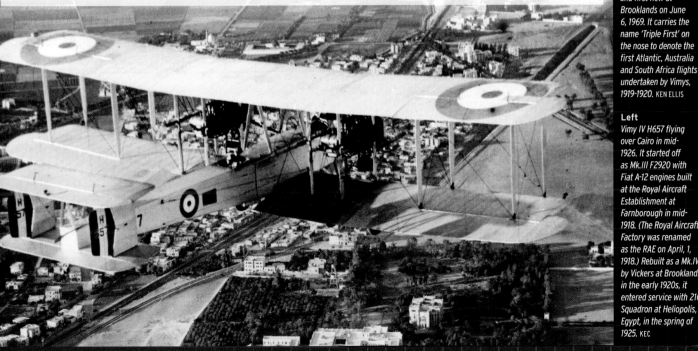

# AVRO ALDERSHOT

## 1924 TO 1926

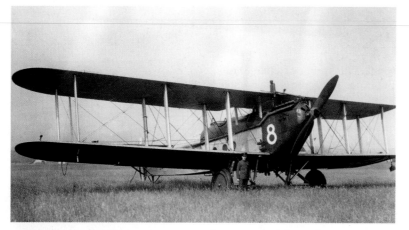

As flight evolved from tenuous adventures by pioneers into a fully fledged form of transport and warfare, an argument raged that was unresolved for decades: one or more engines? Those that thought a solitary powerplant was unsafe were countered by those who believed that two meant there was twice as much to go wrong and any more represented worrisome complexity.

With this and budgetary constraints in mind, the Air Ministry issued Specification 2/20 for a single-engined, long-range bomber. Avro won the day with the huge Aldershot biplane, the first bomber designed for the RAF since the end of the Great War.

The prototype was first flown at Hamble in October 1921, powered by a 650hp (484kW) Rolls-Royce Condor III. As the type was developed, a thundering 16-cylinder X-format 1,000hp Napier Cub was fitted, necessitating a four-wheel undercarriage. The more modest Condor was chosen for production examples.

The Aldershot had a metal-framed fuselage and conventional wooden wings. The 68-foot span was made more manageable in the small hangars of the day as the wings folded to lie alongside the fuselage.

Comparison with other types help put the Aldershot into context and show how little technology advanced at the time. The Aldershot replaced the Vickers Vimy biplane, powered by a pair of 360hp Rolls-Royce Eagle VIIIs. With a 68ft 1in span and a wing area of 1,330sq ft (123.5m2) the Vimy could carry a 2,500lb (1,134kg) bomb load at 100mph for 900 miles (1,448km).

On 650hp, the 68ft span and 1,064sq ft wing area Aldershot took 2,200lb at 110mph for 625 miles. The Aldershot was supplanted by the Handley Page Hyderabad which shaped up as follows: two 450hp Napier Lion IIs, 75ft span, 1,471sq ft wing area, 109mph, 1,100lb of bombs and 500 miles range. Such was progress!

## SPREADING THE WORK

Reflecting the small size of the RAF – around 48 home-based fighter and bomber squadrons – and the nation's parlous financial state, just 15 Aldershots were acquired. All but one served with 99 Squadron at Bircham Newton between July 1924 and April 1926. Then, the fleet was retired to the Home Aircraft Depot at Henlow for spares recovery and scrapping. Throughout the inter-war years the Air Ministry seldom ordered aircraft in large numbers, keeping to modest batches. As well as keeping the Treasury happy, there was a determination to spread the work around the manufacturers, thereby keeping them in business – but only just.

There are several instances of a single unit operating a 'unique' type within this journal: for example, the Fairey Fox with 12 Squadron and the Boulton Paul Sidestrand with 101 Squadron.

For the industry, the development costs of such basic types were relatively modest and there was always the hope that other variants, or exports, would help boost the balance sheets. To this end, Avro mated the wings, undercarriage, forward fuselage and 'tail feathers' of the Aldershot to a new fuselage to create the Andover general purpose transport and ambulance in 1924. The Air Ministry bought four, none of which entered operational service. ◉

### AVRO ALDERSHOT

| | |
|---|---|
| **Type:** | Three-seat day heavy bomber |
| **First flight:** | October 1921, entered service June 1924 |
| **Powerplant:** | One 650hp (484kW) Rolls-Royce Condor III V12 |
| **Dimensions:** | Span 68ft 0in (20.7m), Length 45ft 0in (13.7m) |
| **Weights:** | Empty 6,310lb (2,862kg), All-up 10,950lb (4,966kg) |
| **Max speed:** | 110mph (177km/h) at sea level |
| **Range:** | Endurance 6 hours |
| **Armament:** | One machine gun in nose position, another in dorsal position and another in ventral position. Up to 2,200lb (997kg) of bombs |
| **Replaced:** | Vickers Vimy from 1924 |
| **Taken on charge:** | 15 |
| **Replaced by:** | Handley Page Hyderabad from 1926 |

# VICKERS
# VIRGINIA
## 1924 TO 1941

When 7 Squadron took delivery of it first Virginia III at Bircham Newton in June 1924, the Vimy's reign as the RAF's bomber of choice began to wane. Vickers essentially had come up with a 'Super Vimy', although it represented only a fractional improvement over its predecessor.

In the 1920s new types for the RAF were expected to serve for five or so years, a decade at most. The Virginia was destined to serve with frontline units until 1938, by which time the lumbering biplane was manifestly obsolete. There were ten major versions and by the time the Mk.X appeared in 1928 all it had in common with the prototype was its format. Almost everything had changed: the wing shape, the length, the gun positions and the construction system. The Virginia started as wooden aeroplane; it ended with a metal airframe.

The prototype Virginia, J6856, gave incredible service from its first flight at Brooklands in November 1922, until February 1937 with 215 Squadron at Driffield. Its longevity, and almost constant state of change, is typical of the RAF's Virginias.

Built as a Mk.I in 'silver' dope colour scheme, it morphed into a Mk.III in late 1924, a Mk.VIII in 1925 and reverted to a Mk.VII in 1926 by which time it was in dark green 'night' camouflage. In 1928 J6856 was transformed into an all-metal Mk.X: 11ft 8in (3.55m) longer, 407lb (184kg) heavier and 11mph (17.7km/h) faster than it had been six years before.

During its life, J6856 had three different engine 'fits'. It started with Napier Lion Is of 468hp (349kw), a brief spell with 650hp Rolls-Royce Condor IIIs and finally 500hp Lion Vs.

The Virginia prototype served with four front line units, in turn 9, 7, 10 and 215 Squadrons. It was also detached for test and trials at Martlesham Heath on five

different occasions and with the Royal Aircraft Establishment at Farnborough in mid-1930.

Throughout its evolution J6856 was sent back to Vickers for engine changes, upgrades, refurbishment etc in 12 separate sessions, some lasting a couple of weeks and one for 13 months. During its 171-month flying career, J6856 spent 50-plus months being reworked.

## FIGHTING TOPS

The most visually dramatic modification to J6856 was undertaken in mid-1925. Its fuselage was 'stretched' by 6ft (1.83m) and it was fitted with a pair of so-called 'fighting tops' as an interim Mk.VIII.

While little could be done to increase the speed of the Virginia its defences needed improving – it was vulnerable to rearward attack. The solution was gun positions in streamlined fairings on the

trailing edge of the upper wings. From these fighting tops, the gunners had an uncluttered field of fire.

The gunners reached these precarious-looking compartments by climbing out of the fuselage, through the centre section to emerge out of a hatch onto the top wing. From there they made their way, via grab rails to their 'offices' – all while being battered by a 100mph (160km/h) slipstream.

A more practical answer was achieved with the Mk.IX which featured a gun position in the extreme tail. This was retained in the final version, the metal-

**Left**
*The view, over the shoulder of the front gunner, from the cockpit of a Virginia X of Boscombe Down-based 9 Squadron. The bombers await their turn to take part in a Hendon display in the early 1930s. Aircraft 'S-for-Sugar' carries the name 'King Cerdic of Wessex' on the rear gunner position – he was the first Saxon monarch of Wessex in the 6th century. Several of 9 Squadron's Virginias were named after Wessex kings.*

## VICKERS VIRGINIA X

| | |
|---|---|
| **Type:** | Seven-crew heavy bomber |
| **First flight:** | November 24, 1922, Mk.X entered service January 1928 |
| **Powerplant:** | Two 580hp (432kW) Napier Lion VB W-format 12 cylinder |
| **Dimensions:** | Span 87ft 8in (26.71m), Length 62ft 3in (18.97m) |
| **Weights:** | Empty 9,650lb (4,377kg), All-up 17,600lb (7,983kg) |
| **Max speed:** | 108mph (173km/h) at 5,000ft (1,524m) |
| **Range:** | 985 miles (1,585km) |
| **Armament:** | One machine gun in nose position, two in tail position. Up to 3,000lb (1,360kg) of bombs in bomb bay and under the wing roots |
| **Replaced:** | Vickers Vimy from 1924 |
| **Taken on charge:** | 124, many converted and updated during service |
| **Replaced by:** | HP Heyford from 1934, AW Whitley from 1938 |

**Above**
*Auxiliary Air Force Virginia X J7438 'Isle of Sheppey' of 500 Squadron. Built originally as a Mk.V, this machine served 500 at Manston from January 1934 to January 1936.* KEC

**Below left**
*Virginia X J8330 of 58 Squadron: it flew with the Worthy Down-based unit from mid-1931 until at least the start of 1934.*
© ANDY HAY
www.flyingart.co.uk

framed Mk.X. The last Virginia was delivered to the RAF from Brooklands in November 1932.

## WING WALKERS

Gunners in their lofty fighting tops were not the only 'wing walkers' involved with Virginias. In September 1925 the RAF established the Parachute Test Section (PTS later PT Flight) at Henlow and before long Virginias became the unit's main equipment. The role of the PTS was split between perfecting the still nascent 'art' of parachuting, and teaching people to throw themselves out of a perfectly serviceable aircraft and trust in a silken canopy.

Small wooden platforms were built at the base of the outer rear strut of the lower wing. A parachutist would stand on this, strap himself to the strut and hold on tight! After having climbed to height, the airman would release his ties and jump off the trailing edge of the wing, well clear of the tail surfaces. (PTF continued its work all the way through to 1950, using Handley Page Halifaxes and Douglas Dakotas.)

On September 4, 1941 Virginia X J7434 took off from Henlow on another parachute testing sortie, a job it had been carrying out since December 1938. At the end of the flight, the big biplane undershot on approach, tore through telegraph wires and came to an abrupt halt. The venerable bomber was not worth repairing. It was the last of its kind and the anachronistic Virginia slipped into extinction. ◎

J8330

## "The Virginia was destined to serve with frontline units until 1938, by which time the lumbering biplane was manifestly obsolete."

# FAIREY
# BIPLANES
## 1924 TO 1941

Floatplanes for the Royal Naval Air Service were the staple of Fairey Aviation's output from its factory at Hayes in the later years of the Great War. In late 1917 Fairey produced what it called the Series III, a large two-seat bomber, which transformed the fledgling company into a major player in the industry.

Developments of this design continued all the way through to the all-metal IIIF. Never given a name, the last Fairey IIIs were built in 1932 and examples served on as late as 1939. The Series IIIs were general-purpose types, but the experience led to Fairey branching out into fighters and bombers.

In March 1923 the company flew the prototype Fawn, initially intended as an army co-operation type for the RAF. The Air Ministry chopped and changed its requirements and the type was accepted – as the first all-new light bomber for the RAF – to replace the venerable de Havilland DH.9A. Powered by a 470hp (360kW) Napier Lion V, the Fawn could carry a bomb load of 460lb (208kg).

When production ended in 1926 a total of 74 Fawns had been built in four versions. Air Ministry whims infuriated the company's leading light, Richard Fairey, and influenced his later thinking; the most obvious was the sudden need not to place fuel

tanks within the fuselage, to reduce the risk of fire. A streamlined tank was placed, port and starboard, on top of the inboard section of upper wing – a cynic at the time observing they were "perfectly positioned to rain ignited petrol down upon the crew".

The first unit to accept Fawns for service was 12 Squadron at Andover in March 1924. The type left frontline use in December 1926, largely replaced by Hawker Horsleys, but in 12's case with the Fox – see below. Fawns also served with Auxiliary Air Force units until 1929.

### LEADING THE WAY
The Schneider Trophy, seeking the fastest seaplanes, was hosted by Britain in 1923. Richard Fairey was wide-eyed at the sleek Curtiss CR-3 biplanes, powered by Curtiss D-12 V12-format engines, which won the competition at a sizzling 177mph (284km/h), and a fact-finding tour of the USA led to a licence agreement for the D-12, Curtiss-Reed adjustable-pitch propellers and patented wing sections.

Tired of Air Ministry meddling, Fairey was going to build a private venture bomber that would make the

## FAIREY FOX

| | |
|---|---|
| **Type:** | Two-seat light day bomber |
| **First flight:** | January 3, 1925; entered service June 1926 |
| **Powerplant:** | One 480hp (358kW) Curtiss D-12 V12 |
| **Dimensions:** | Span 37ft 8in (11.47m), Length 28ft 03in (8.61m) |
| **Weights:** | Empty 2,610lb (1,183kg), All-up 4,170lb (1,891kg) |
| **Max speed:** | 150mph (45.7km/h) at 10,000ft (3,048m) |
| **Range:** | 500 miles (804km) |
| **Armament:** | One machine gun firing through propeller arc, another in rear position. Up to 460lb (208kg) of bombs |
| **Replaced:** | Fairey Fawn – served only with 12 Squadron |
| **Taken on charge:** | 28 |
| **Replaced by:** | Hawker Hart |

Fawn look pedestrian. Belgian-born designer Marcelle Lobelle came up with the Fox, the first taking to the air on January 3, 1925. It did everything the Fawn could do, but was nearly 50mph (80km/h) faster – an incredible leap in performance.

As the Fox wasn't officially sanctioned, it would be difficult to get it accepted. The Chief of the Air Staff, ACM Sir Hugh Trenchard, visited the Fairey test airfield at Northolt on July 28, 1925, when chief test pilot Norman Macmillan put the Fox through its paces. The story goes that Trenchard was so impressed he ordered a squadron of Foxes from Richard Fairey there and then.

Trenchard was true to his word: Fairey built 28 of the revolutionary bombers, but no more (although a single-seat fighter development, the Firefly, was produced for Belgium). The only operational unit with Foxes was 12 Squadron which took its first examples in June 1926, some of which were re-engined with Rolls-Royce Kestrels, before they gave way to the equally ground-breaking Hawker Hart in 1931.

## FACE OF THE FOX
Fairey is believed to have lost a fortune developing the Fox. The company was fighting entrenched thinking from the ministry and the rest of the industry: the aircraft circumvented procedure and used a foreign engine (Fairey intended to build the D-12 in Britain as the Felix, but with such a small order, it was not economical).

There can be no doubt that Hawker's Sydney Camm was enthused by the potential of the thinking that had brought about the Fox. Even the Air Ministry took notice, realising that, occasionally, manufacturers might be more in tune with cutting-edge technology.

Foxes outshone all the 'opposition' in every exercise or demonstration they attended. Their success, and unique use by the unit, provided the inspiration for 12 Squadron's badge – the face of a *Vulpes vulpes*, the red fox. Approved by King George VI in February 1937, the badge had the appropriate motto 'Leads the Field'.

After the Fairey Fox, 12 Squadron went on to operate Hawker Harts and Hinds (from 1931), Fairey Battles (1938), Vickers Wellingtons (1940), Avro Lancasters (1942), Avro Lincolns (1946), English Electric Canberras (1952), Avro Vulcans (1962) and Hawker Siddeley Buccaneers (1969).

Its current equipment is the Panavia Tornado, which was adopted in 1993, and 12 Squadron will be one of the last to fly the swing-wing strike aircraft.

## GORDON'S ALIVE
The final development of the Series III abandoned the faithful Napier Lion engine and adopted the Armstrong Siddeley Panther radial. As such it was referred to as the Series IIIF Mk.V for the RAF and the Mk.VI for the Fleet Air Arm (FAA). The prototype, a conversion of a IIIF Mk.IV, appeared in April 1929.

It was high time to drop the 'Series III' label and the new version was called Gordon by the RAF and Seal by the FAA – the RAF name reviving memories of 19th century warrior Major-General Charles George Gordon.

Gordons entered service with the re-formed 40 Squadron at Upper Heyford in April 1931, and were widely used in the Middle East, replacing the last of the Bristol F.2b Fighters. The last British-based Gordons retired in November 1937.

The final Gordons rolled out of the factory in 1934, completing an astounding 17 years of manufacturing Series III derivatives. During the Iraq insurrection in May 1941, the beleaguered 4 Flying Training School at Habbaniya still had some Gordons on hand to quell German-backed hostilities. ◉

**Above**
*Built in 1931 as a Series III Mk.IVB, K1776 was converted into a Gordon in 1932. It was issued to 35 Squadron at Bircham Newton in July 1932 and moved with the unit to the Sudan in late 1935. It crashed at 35's base at Gebeit, close to the Red Sea coast, on January 27, 1936.*
© ANDY HAY
www.flyingart.co.uk

**Above**
*A gunner/observer takes a camera from a member of the ground crew ready for stowage in his compartment on board a Gordon of 40 Squadron at Upper Heyford in 1931. Note the externally mounted Vickers machine gun.*

# HANDLEY PAGE
# HYDERABAD

## 1925 TO 1935

When 99 Squadron received its first Hyderabad at Bircham Newton in December 1925, there was some relief the unit was once again operating a twin. For 16 months prior to that, 99 had been flying the huge, single-engined Avro Aldershot. Prior to the Avro, 99 Squadron flew the reliable and well-liked Vickers Vimy – the biplanes that had conquered the Atlantic non-stop.

It is reasonable to conclude that the Vimy, first flown in 1917, was well outclassed by the Hyderabad. Not so, only in speed did the Handley Page bomber win out, with a maximum speed of 109mph (175km/h) is was 9mph faster. The Vimy had a range of 900 miles (1,448km) and a bomb load of 2,500lb (1,134kg); eclipsing the Hyderabad by 400 miles and 1,400lb respectively.

What sort of progress was this? Alongside the Vimy, Handley Page had been developing the O/400 bomber, and both were intended to take the war to the cities of Germany – ideally all the way to Berlin. This was to bring the German population into the front line in the same way

that Zeppelin airships and Gotha bombers had for the people of Britain. The Admiralty had told Handley Page "a bloody paralyser of an aeroplane" was needed.

By 1925 things had changed and the technological advances brought on by the extreme needs of war had receded. The Great War had become known as the 'War to end all wars' and its ferocity and carnage had left Europe in a state of shock. The Versailles Treaty of 1919 had inflicted

swingeing sanctions on Germany, and great faith was being placed in the League of Nations which came into being in January 1920 to police disputes between countries.

British foreign policy assumed there would not be a major war involving Britain or its empire for all of the 1920s and well into the 1930s. The Hyderabad did not need

long range, or high performance; it was there to present a deterrent and keep aircrew proficient in the art of bombing. None of the nations across the English Channel or the North Sea had an aircraft that rivalled it.

The most action the Hyderabad was expected to face would be against dissident tribes in the Middle East or Afghan warlords in the North-West Frontier of India. The section on the Hawker Horsley, explains a little about how the RAF named its aircraft

### HANDLEY PAGE HYDERABAD

| | |
|---|---|
| **Type:** | Four-crew heavy bomber |
| **First flight:** | October 1923, entered service December 1925 |
| **Powerplant:** | Two 500hp (373kW) Napier Lion V W-format, 12-cylinder |
| **Dimensions:** | Span 75ft 0in (22.8m), Length 59ft 2in (18.0m) |
| **Weights:** | Empty 8,910lb (4,041kg), All-up 13,590lb (6,164kg) |
| **Range:** | 500 miles (804km) |
| **Max speed:** | 109mph (175km/h) at sea level |
| **Armament:** | Three machine guns, in nose, dorsal and ventral positions. Up to 1,100lb (498kg) of bombs |
| **Replaced:** | Avro Aldershot, Vickers Vimy |
| **Taken on charge:** | 44 with conversions to Hinaidi |
| **Replaced by:** | Handley Page Heyford |

# AND HINAIDI

## "The most action the Hyderabad was expected to face would be against dissident tribes in the Middle East or Afghan warlords in the North-West Frontier of India."

in this period; Hyderabad is a city in central southern India. The improved Hinaidi was named after another hotspot, a town near Baghdad in Iraq.

### FROM INDIA TO IRAQ

Handley Page developed the Hyderabad from the all-new W.8 civil airliner of 1919 and the prototype bomber had its maiden flight in October 1923. It was to be the last British 'heavy' using a primarily wooden airframe. As well as the nose gun position – known as 'the pulpit' – there was a dorsal position and an innovative ventrally mounted gun to protect the vulnerable underside.

Apart from 99 Squadron, the only other frontline unit to fly the Hyderabad was 10 Squadron, which re-formed at Upper Heyford in January 1928, and worked up on the new Handley Page. The Auxiliary Air Force unit, 503 Squadron at Waddington, flew Hyderabads from February 1929.

On March 29, 1927 the replacement for the Hyderabad was flown for the first time. This was the Hinaidi, an improved version of its predecessor: indeed, the prototype was converted from a Hyderabad. The Lions were replaced by 450hp (335kw) Bristol Jupiter radials and the Mk.IIs that began to appear in 1930 had all-metal structures.

All three units that had operated Hyderabads – 10, 99 and 503 Squadrons – took on Hinaidis, the first being Upper Heyford-based 99 in October 1929. Hinaidis left frontline usage in late 1933 when the Handley Page Heyford took over. At Waddington, 503 Squadron gave up its Hinaidis in October 1935, taking on Westland Wallaces.

Forty-four Hyderabads had been built and the RAF received 45 Hinaidis, a mixture of conversions and new-builds. Three transport versions of the Hinaidi were also built, serving in India between 1931 and 1934. Originally given the name Chitral – after a city in present-day northern Pakistan, they adopted Clive, in honour of Major-General Robert Clive, the 18th century 'Clive of India'. ◉

# HAWKER
# HORSLEY
## 1926 TO 1935

With the Great War still raging, Lt Col James G Weir, Controller of the Technical Department of the Ministry of Munitions, issued a document on July 8, 1918 outlining how the new Royal Air Force would name its aircraft. Weir – who became a pioneer of British rotorcraft from the mid-1920s – was anxious to establish some consistency.

As regards single-engined land-based or deck-landing types, single-seaters were to take the names of reptiles or birds, but not snakes or predatory avians. Single-engined two- or three-seaters could adopt mammals, except for cats. The snakes, raptors and felines were the exclusive domain of engine builders.

Multi-engined machines up to 11,000lb (4,989kg) all-up weight could choose towns in England or Wales. Above that figure, places in Scotland and Ireland could be picked – how's that for regionalism! Later, locations in the colonies were added.

The 'system' was occasionally revised and today the RAF still gives its aircraft names, not numbers. There have been many exceptions to the rules of the day and one of the greatest was a biplane from Hawker. It revelled in the name of a stately home that had been owned by the company's chief, Thomas Sopwith!

To be fair, it was originally proposed that the new type be called Kingston, after the Hawker factory and headquarters. Horsley was chosen to honour Horsley Towers, a huge early 19th century manor house set in nearly 3,000 acres of land alongside the hamlet of East Horsley in Surrey.

Aged 30, Sopwith successfully bid a whopping £150,000 (£16·5 million in present-day values) for the place in 1918 and he poured money in to modernise it. In September 1920 Sopwith Aviation and Engineering was liquidated and 'Tommy' was forced to sell Horsley Towers. But the name was to take to the skies with Sopwith's new business, Hawker.

## SHORT SERVICE

Initially conceived to be a day bomber, as development of the Horsley progressed, it was adapted into a torpedo carrier. The prototype first flew in 1925.

As was commonplace in the 1920s, the design went through an evolution as the RAF took on charge 113 Horsleys between 1926 and 1931. After ten all-wooden Mk.Is, the 67 Mk.IIs featured a metal-framed forward fuselage. The final 36 Horsleys had an all-metal structure but oddly these never received the more logical Mk.III designation.

The big biplane enjoyed some export success: to Denmark – where it was called the Dantorp – and to Greece.

The first pure bomber examples for the RAF were issued to 100 Squadron at Grantham in August 1926, replacing Fairey Fawns. Horsleys bowed out of British frontline service with 33 Squadron at Eastchurch

## HAWKER HORSLEY II

| | |
|---|---|
| **Type:** | Two-seat day/torpedo bomber |
| **First flight:** | 1925, entered service August 1926 |
| **Powerplant:** | One 665hp (496kW) Rolls-Royce Condor IIIA V12 |
| **Dimensions:** | Span 56ft 6in (17.22m), Length 38ft 10in (11.83m) |
| **Weights:** | Empty 4,958lb (2,248kg), All-up 9,271lb (4,205kg) |
| **Max speed:** | 113mph (181km/h) at 10,000ft (3,048m) in bomber role |
| **Range:** | 900 miles (1,448km) |
| **Armament:** | One 0.303in machine gun firing through propeller arc, another in dorsal position. Up to 1,500lb (680kg) of bombs or one 2,150lb (975) torpedo |
| **Replaced:** | De Havilland DH.9A and Fairey Fawn from 1926 |
| **Taken on charge:** | 113 |
| **Replaced by:** | Westland Wapiti from 1928, Hawker Hart from 1930, Vickers Vildebeest from 1932 |

when it converted to Hawker Harts in the spring of 1930. The special reserve 504 (County of Nottingham) Squadron was formed at Hucknall in 1928 and the following year took delivery of Horsleys. They were traded in for Westland Wallaces in March 1934.

At Leuchars, the Coast Defence Torpedo Bomber Flight started working up on Horsleys from July 1928 and became operational, as 36 Squadron at Donibristle, in September. In late 1930 the unit relocated to Seletar, Singapore, to boost British presence at the newly completed naval base. Vickers Vildebeests replaced 36 Squadron's Horsleys in July 1935.

## UPSTAGED

The cavernous fuselage and large wings of the Horsley made it ideal to be turned into a flying fuel tank for ultra-long range sorties. A non-stop flight to India to show off British aeronautical prowess and to do a spot

of 'flag waving' was a very tempting prospect.

Hawker prepared two Horsley Specials, J8607 and J8608. Standard fuel tankage was 276 Imp gal (1,254 lit) and this was boosted to 1,320 in the wings and within the fuselage. This got the take-off weight up to an incredible 14,000lb (6,350kg) – just shy of that of the twin-engined Handley Page Hinaidi heavy bomber.

That explains why J8607 just missed the boundary wall on take-off from Cranwell at 10:38 hours (all times local) on May 20, 1927. The Horsley was piloted by Flt Lt Charles 'Roddy' Carr – later Air Marshal Sir Roderick Carr – and navigated by Flt Lt L E M Gillman. The biplane was observed over southern Germany, heading for the Alps. Then there were no more sightings.

Abeam Bandar Abbas in Iran, a fuel blockage ended the adventure. After 34 hours airborne, they had achieved a world record distance of 3,419 miles (5,502km). Carr made an approach

to what he thought was a flat stretch of sand, but it turned out to be the Persian Gulf at its most tranquil.

At 21:08 on May 21 J8607 settled into the water and the crew climbed on to the top wing and hoped for rescue. They were picked up the following day.

Another heavily laden aircraft had struggled into the air on May 20, clearing telephone wires by a matter of feet. The time was 07:52, the venue Roosevelt Field, New York. Piloting the single-engined Ryan NYP, *Spirit of St Louis*, was Charles Lindbergh. He touched down at Le Bourget, Paris, at 22:22 on the 21st, having taken 33 hours 30 minutes to fly 3,590 miles to achieve the first solo non-stop crossing of the Atlantic.

Paris time was three hours ahead of the clock in Bandar Abbas. Drenched and defeated, Carr and Gillman could not have known it, but their record stood for just a couple of hours. Their endeavours were lost in the tsunami of press coverage that greeted the 'Lone Eagle' – Lindbergh.

Undaunted, Carr was at the controls of the second Horsley Special, J8608, as it departed Cranwell on June 16, 1927, again bound for India. In the back was Flt Lt P H Mackworth. An oil leak in the Rolls-Royce Condor IIIA – named after a bird of prey – necessitated a precautionary landing at Martlesham Heath.

Repaired, J8608 and Carr set off again, on August 2, with Fg Off E C Dearth navigating. They got as far as Austria where another ditching, this time into the far more hostile River Danube near Linz, was required. Workmen on the bank dragged the two men out of the wreck: Carr was merely shaken, Dearth was badly injured, but made a full recovery. The India expedition was quietly shelved. ◉

**"Abeam Bandar Abbas in Iran, a fuel blockage ended the adventure. ...Carr made an approach to what he thought was a flat stretch of sand, but it turned out to be the Persian Gulf at its most tranquil."**

# BOULTON AND PAUL
# 'STRANDS'

## 1929 TO 1940

**Right**
*Publicity photograph of air and ground crews of 101 Squadron, briefing and maintaining Sidestrands "on exercise on the east coast of Scotland", circa 1931. Note how the Bristol Jupiter VIII radial on the aircraft in the foreground is hinged to allow engineers access to the ancillaries.*

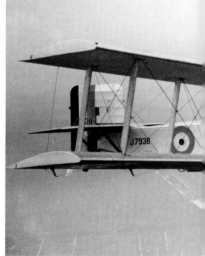

People with no knowledge of RAF bombers, but with a love of the north Norfolk coast will immediately associate with Overstrand and Sidestrand. Just to the east of Cromer lie a small township and a village with those names. Boulton and Paul (BP) had its factory at Mousehold northeast of Norwich and someone with influence clearly had a soft spot for the 'twin' coastal settlements.

Primarily a woodworking enterprise, the company sold off its small aviation arm in 1934, which became Boulton Paul Aircraft Ltd, and two years later re-located to Pendeford, Wolverhampton.

Several attempts had been made to break into the bomber market, but without success. With Specification 9/24, setting down the requirements for the first RAF bomber to be designated as 'medium', the company at last got a contract.

Powered by a pair of 425hp (317kW) Bristol Jupiter VIs the prototype first flew in March 1926 and the all-metal biplane was an immediate sensation. It was capable of rolls and loops that would fool an RAF fighter attempting a practice interception. Yet it was easy to fly and very stable, making it a pilot and a bomb aimer favourite.

Despite this, only 18 production-standard Mk.IIs were ordered, all going to 101 Squadron at Bircham Newton at the western extremity of Norfolk. With Sidestrands, 101 excelled in exercises and competitions and an improved version would be equally well greeted. Along with the Fairey Fox light bomber, the RAF was beginning to modernise.

### ZIPPED UP

In 1927 BP began testing the Bittern twin-engined 'bomber destroyer', which featured machine guns in barbettes that could be mechanically rotated to fire upwards. It was not ordered into production. Undaunted, BP built up expertise in gun turrets and powered control systems.

The Sidestrand was nearly 40mph (64km/h) faster than the Handley Page Hyderabad. Its gunners, particularly those in the nose, complained that the slipstream was preventing accurate aiming. Designer John Dudley North decided the enhanced Sidestrand would protect the gunner and ease the physical effort required.

The turret's single Lewis gun was manually elevated or depressed. A hydraulic ram, connected to the gunner's seat, raised or lowered him so he could continue to look along the barrel to the sight.

The cylindrical, glazed, cupola had a vertical slot to allow the gun to train up or down. To prevent a howling gale coming through the slot, the machine gun's barrel was connected to a long zip fastener, stitched to rubberised fabric. As the gun moved up or down the zip would open above the gun and close up behind it.

As the gun was pushed to port or starboard, switches detected the movement and a pneumatic motor moved the turret in the required direction.

The new machine also featured a fully enclosed and heated cockpit for the pilot and a limited-authority auto-pilot. The big rudder took a lot of 'boot' to move, so a large servo-rudder was mounted on out-riggers attached to its trailing edge to lower control loads. The Bristol Jupiters were replaced by more powerful Pegasus IIM3s.

The bomber had the first power-operated, fully enclosed turret, to be fitted on an RAF aircraft. This was well ahead of the turrets being developed by the Nash and Thompson at Yate, but the Gloucestershire company

## BOULTON PAUL OVERSTRAND

| | |
|---|---|
| **Type:** | Three-crew medium bomber |
| **First flight:** | August 1933, entered service June 1936 |
| **Powerplant:** | Two 580hp (432kW) Bristol Pegasus IIM3 radials |
| **Dimensions:** | Span 72ft 0in (21.9m), Length 46ft 0in (14.0m) |
| **Weights:** | Empty 7,936lb (3,599kg), All-up 12,000lb (5,443kg) |
| **Max speed:** | 153mph (246km/h) at 6,500ft (1,981m) |
| **Range:** | 545 miles (877km) |
| **Armament:** | One machine gun in nose turret, one in dorsal and one in ventral position. Up to 1,600lb (725kg) of bombs |
| **Replaced:** | Boulton Paul Sidestrand |
| **Taken on charge:** | 24, and conversions from Sidestrands |
| **Replaced by:** | Bristol Blenheim Is in 1938 |

**Above left**
*Overstrand K4561 was delivered to 101 Squadron at Bicester in May 1936. It was withdrawn from use in August 1938 and scrapped the following year. The large rudder servo-tab, mounted on the rudder, was a means of lessening control loads.*
© ANDY HAY
www.flyingart.co.uk

**Left**
*The Sidestrand prototype, J7938, served on and off with 101 Squadron during its service life, 1926-1934. In between it had periods back with Boulton Paul, the Aeroplane and Armament Experimental Establishment at Martlesham Heath, and the Royal Aircraft Establishment at Farnborough.* KEC

**Left**
*Overstrand J9815 started life as a Sidestrand II in 1929, serving with 101 Squadron. It was rebuilt as a Sidestrand and re-entered service with 101 in January 1935. It was written off following a crash at North Coates on September 9, 1935.* KEC

overhauled BP and become the top manufacturer of the RAF's turrets for the 'heavies' of World War Two.

### END OF THE LINE

Converted from a Sidestrand, and initially known as the Sidestrand Mk.V before Overstrand was settled upon, the prototype had its maiden flight in August 1933. The first deliveries were made to 101 Squadron, by then at Bicester, in January 1935. Oddly another Bicester-based unit, the newly re-formed 144 Squadron,

operated a quartet of Overstrands during the first two months of 1937, before standardising on Hawker Audaxes.

Overstrands were retired from frontline use in June 1938 when Bristol Blenheim Is were adopted. A handful were still on charge with 10 Bombing and Gunnery School at Warmwell, in early 1940.

After the disastrous Defiant turret fighter, BP became an

efficient sub-contractor during World War Two. Post-war BP returned to designing aircraft, but in 1957 it completed its last aircraft to concentrate on powered control units of increasing sophistication.

The name Boulton Paul was dispensed with in 1969 and today the enterprise is part of the Moog Group. At the forefront of servo motors and controls, the company can trace its roots back to the RAF's first turrets. ◉

## "The Sidestrand was capable of rolls and loops that would fool an RAF fighter attempting a practice interception. Yet it was easy to fly and very stable, making it a pilot and a bomb aimer favourite."

# HAWKER
# HART AND HIND

## 1928 TO 1943

**Right**
Hart (India) K2096 of 39 Squadron, based at Risalpur from November 1931. It stayed in India and was written off in a crash while serving with 1 Service Flying Training School at Ambala, northern India, on August 3, 1942.
PETE WEST

**Right**
Hind K5466 of 40 Squadron heading up an immaculate line-up with Handley Page Heyfords behind. This machine served Abingdon-based 40 Squadron from April 1936 to August 1938.
KEC

While the Fairey Fox of 1925 was revolutionary, it raised opposition and prejudices in the Air Ministry, the RAF and elements of the aviation industry. The Fox helped to convince the Hawker designer, Sydney Camm, of the way forward and it was Hart-shaped.

The Hart was arguably the most important aircraft to enter RAF service in the early 1930s. Its influence cannot be over estimated.

A two-seat day bomber, which was faster than contemporary fighters, the Hawker company knew it had the basis of a series of warplanes. Exploiting the design's speed, it began a two-pronged programme – single-seater fighters and two-seaters capable of fulfilling a wide range of roles.

The fighters evolved as the Fury for the RAF and the Nimrod for the Fleet Air Arm (FAA). These owed constructional technique and design philosophy to the Hart, but were essentially clean-sheet designs.

The Hart's airframe was morphed into a family, including a dedicated trainer and its own replacement the Hind. It also spawned the Demon two-seat fighter; the Audax army co-operation version and its replacement, the Hector, the Hardy 'colonial' general-purpose type for the RAF and the Osprey reconnaissance two-seater for the FAA. There was also a plethora of export versions with all manner of engine options.

This success transformed Hawker into the industry leader: indeed, from the late 1920s, the RAF was often referred to as the 'Hawker Air Force'. Such was the status

of the company that its chief, Thomas Sopwith, masterminded the acquisition of Armstrong Whitworth, Avro and Gloster in 1935 to form the Hawker Siddeley Group.

## "Combined production of Harts and Hinds surpassed all other bomber types taken on charge by the RAF since 1919 other than the venerable, much rebuilt and revived DH.9A."

### HAWKER HART

| | |
|---|---|
| **Type:** | Two-seat light bomber |
| **First flight:** | June 1928, entered service January 1930 |
| **Powerplant:** | One 525hp (391kW) Rolls-Royce Kestrel IB V12 |
| **Dimensions:** | Span 37ft 3in (11.35m), Length 29ft 4in (9.04m) |
| **Weights:** | Empty 2,530lb (1,147kg), All-up 4,554lb (2,065kg) |
| **Max speed:** | 184mph (296km/h) at 10,000ft (3,048m) |
| **Range:** | 430 miles (691km) |
| **Armament:** | One machine gun firing through propeller arc, another in dorsal position. Up to 500lb (226kg) of bombs |
| **Replaced:** | Fairey Gordon, Hawker Horsley, Westland Wapiti and Wallace from 1930 |
| **Taken on charge:** | 459, sub-contracts to Armstrong Whitworth, Gloster and Vickers |
| **Replaced by:** | Hawker Hind, Demon and Bristol Blenheim from 1936 |

### RED DEER DUO

After a fierce competition with Avro and de Havilland, Hawker's prototype Hart – first flown in 1928 – earned its first contract with the RAF. That was for 15, but was

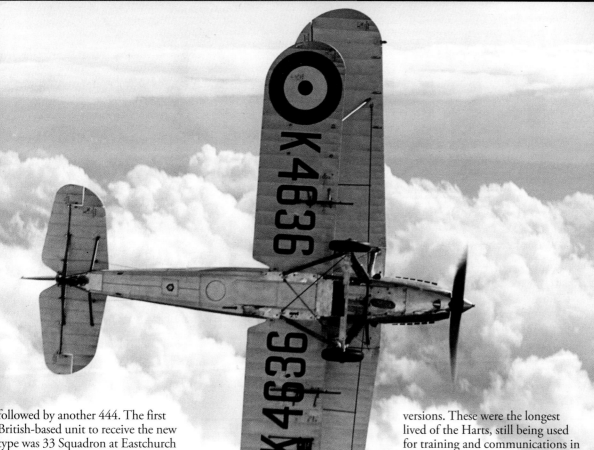

followed by another 444. The first British-based unit to receive the new type was 33 Squadron at Eastchurch in January 1930, replacing Hawker Horsleys.

Two sub-variants were created, the Hart (India) and the Hart (Special) optimised for service in the North-West Frontier and in the Middle East and East Africa respectively. At Risalpur – near Peshawar in present-day Pakistan – 39 Squadron traded in its Westland Wapitis for Harts in November 1931. The first of the type in the Middle East supplanted Fairey IIIFs with 45 Squadron at Helwan, Egypt, in September 1935.

Harts were also ideal for the Special Reserve and Auxiliary Air Force units. At Hendon, 601 (County of London) Squadron equipped with them as early as February 1933.

The improved Hind took over British-based operational units from 1936 and the 'auxiliaries' gave up Harts by 1938.

The Hart Trainer was introduced from April 1932, and 473 were built from new with upwards of 70 conversions of standard bomber versions. These were the longest lived of the Harts, still being used for training and communications in the Middle East in 1943.

A Hart is a stag (male) red deer and for the Hart's replacement, the name Hind, a female red deer, was chosen. The prototype Hind had its debut in September 1934. It featured many refinements picked up as the rest of the Hart family developed, but the most obvious one was a supercharged Rolls-Royce Kestrel V giving it an extra 115hp over its predecessor.

On New Year's Eve 1935, Hind K4637 was delivered to the re-formed 21 Squadron at Bircham Newton: it was the first to join an operational unit. Hinds were removed from the frontline in May 1939, with Bristol Blenheims, Fairey Battles and Handley Page Hampdens taking over.

It was not until November 1939 that the Auxiliary Air Force gave up its Hinds; 613 (City of Manchester) Squadron at Odiham sticking to Hawker biplanes by adopting Audaxes. As with the Hart trainer, versions of the Hind enjoyed longevity up to at least 1942.

When the last Hind was rolled out in June 1938 a total of 528 had been manufactured for the RAF, including 20 from-new trainer versions. Combined production of Harts and Hinds surpassed all other bomber types taken on charge by the RAF since 1919, other than the venerable, much rebuilt and revived DH.9A. ◉

**Left**
*The first production Hind, K4636, cavorting for publicity photos in September 1935. It spent its early years on tests and trials work. Converted to a Hind (T) trainer in 1939, it was handed on to the South African Air Force the following year.*

**Below left**
*The RAF Museum has a trio of classic Hawker biplanes: Hart G-ABMR, flown as a demonstrator and later by the unofficial 'heritage flight' by Hawker, until donated in 1972; Armstrong Whitworth-built Hart Trainer K4972, donated by the Solway Group of Aviation Enthusiasts in 1963, and Hind (Afghan) acquired from Kabul in 1968. Illustrated is G-ABMR 'flying' within Hendon's 'Milestones of Flight' hall, in the colours of 'J9941' of Netheravon-based 57 Squadron, in late 1931.*
RAF MUSEUM WWW. rafmuseum.org

# VICKERS VILDEBEEST

## 1932 TO 1942

| VICKERS VILDEBEEST III | |
| --- | --- |
| Type: | Three-seat day torpedo-bomber / general purpose |
| First flight: | April 1928, Mk.I entered service November 1932 |
| Powerplant: | One 635hp (473kW) Bristol Pegasus IIM3 radial |
| Dimensions: | Span 49ft 0in (14.9m), Length 36ft 8in (11.17m) |
| Weights: | Empty 4,773lb (2,165kg), All-up 8,500lb (3,855kg) |
| Max speed: | 137mph (220km/h) at 10,000ft (3,048m) |
| Range: | 1,250 miles (2,011km) |
| Armament: | One machine gun firing through propeller arc, another in dorsal position. One 1,870lb (848kg) torpedo, or up to 1,000lb (453kg) of bombs |
| Replaced: | Hawker Horsley |
| Taken on charge: | 169, Mks I to IV |
| Replaced by: | Bristol Beaufort during 1940 |

*Below right*
*A line of camouflaged and coded Vildebeests of 100 Squadron at Kota Baharu, eastern Malaya, in mid-1941.*
*Below*
*An 'erk' cranking over the Bristol Pegasus radial of a Seletar-based Vildebeest, circa 1935. Note how part of the nose section folds down to provide a ledge to stand on.*
*BOTH KEC*

When Britain went to war on September 3, 1939 the RAF Coastal Command's only combat capable torpedo-bombers were Vildebeest biplanes. Technical problems with the Bristol Beaufort meant that it was November before any were available for squadron use and another five months before the modern twins were ready for 'ops'.

The big biplanes were used for coastal patrol in Britain until 42 Squadron stood down at Bircham Newton in April 1940 and received Beauforts. In the Far East, 36 and 100 Squadrons were responsible for repelling any maritime threat to Singapore from Japan.

Vildebeests were never used in anger from British bases. The biplanes were in action in Malaya from the moment Japanese forces invaded on December 8, 1941, suffering terrible losses.

Named after the African gnu, or vildebeeste in Afrikaans, the RAF opted for the simpler Vildebeest, without the final 'e', in 1934. The prototype of the big Vickers biplane had its maiden flight in April 1928 and 169 were built, in four different versions.

Replacing the Hawker Horsley, the Vildebeest first entered service with 100 Squadron at Donibristle in November 1932. The unit was shipped to Singapore as part of the beefing up of the naval base's defences and was ready for duty at Seletar in January 1934. The resident 36 Squadron retired its Horsleys in July 1935 and converted to Vildebeests.

## SEALED ORDERS

At 11:15 hours local on September 3, 1939, Britain declared war on Germany. A day later, 6,800 miles (10,840km) to the east, the seriousness of the world situation was felt at Seletar. A 100 Squadron Association pamphlet relates that a film being shown in the station cinema was interrupted. A notice flashed on the screen ordering all personnel of 'A' and 'B' Flights of 36 Squadron and 'B' Flight of 100 Squadron to report to their hangars immediately. There is a note that those that got up and left did not get a refund!

Three Vildebeests of 100 Squadron were being prepared: K6384 (Flt Lt Smith, the flight leader), K6385 (Plt Off Richardson) and K6379 (Plt Off Davis). Each aircraft was to carry two more crew members, a mixture of wireless operator/gunners, fitters and armourers.

The commanding officer, Sqn Ldr R N McKern, set a sombre tone, explaining that the unit was on a war footing and wished the men good luck. The document takes up the story: "The three aircraft became airborne at 09:45 hours local on September 5, 1939, just 39 hours and

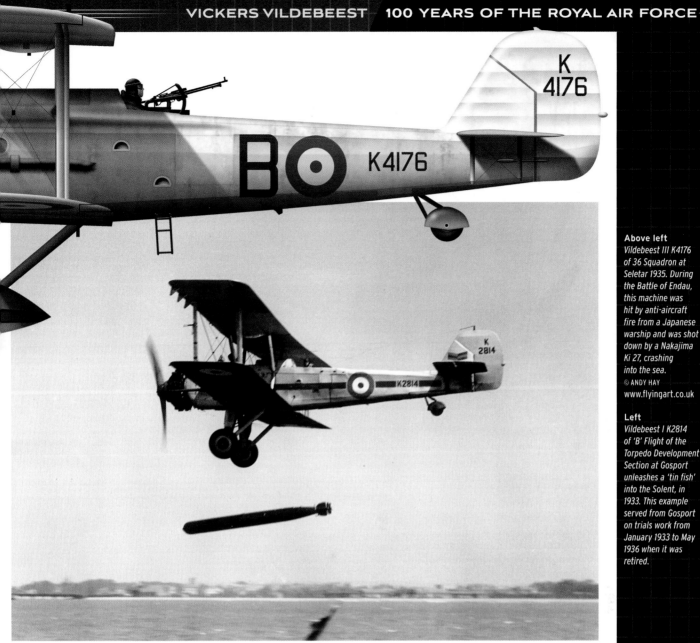

**Above left**
*Vildebeest III K4176 of 36 Squadron at Seletar 1935. During the Battle of Endau, this machine was hit by anti-aircraft fire from a Japanese warship and was shot down by a Nakajima Ki 27, crashing into the sea.*
© ANDY HAY
www.flyingart.co.uk

**Left**
*Vildebeest I K2814 of 'B' Flight of the Torpedo Development Section at Gosport unleashes a 'tin fish' into the Solent, in 1933. This example served from Gosport on trials work from January 1933 to May 1936 when it was retired.*

## "While attacking a Japanese ship during the intense naval engagement off Endau... K6379 was seen to dive into the sea. It was one of 13 of the torpedo-bombers lost that day."

10 minutes after war was declared...

"As soon as the aerodrome was cleared, the pilots opened their sealed envelopes and then told their crews that their destination was Kepala Batas, north of Alor Star. [On the western coast of the Malay Peninsula, 20 miles from the border with Siam, today's Thailand.] The aircraft set course for the northwest tip of Malaya and a loose formation was adopted. The flight took 4 hours 30 minutes and proved to be uneventful."

After 'tiffin' at the government rest house at Kepala Batas, around 16:00, the nine men: "All got busy unpacking and 'hunking' around bombs, 112- and 250-pounders, both general purpose and armour piercing, which were stored there for emergency use. There were no trolleys nor any means

of moving these bombs – only brute strength and sweat!

"Each bomb was in its own wooden crate which was screwed, not nailed, together. The bombs were man-handled to rows some distance from the aircraft and covered with tarpaulin sheets. They were completely safe – they hoped – and the fuzes were locked up well away from both the bombs and the machines, in the rest house. There were no torpedoes.

"Fifteen days later those nine men, with their Vildebeests, saw Seletar again." The men of 36 and 100 Squadrons were thrown into the front line from December 1941 fighting rear guard action before Singapore fell to the Japanese.

The three aircraft that deployed to Kepala Batas on September 5, 1939

illustrate the fate of the Vildebeest force. While attacking a Japanese ship during the intense naval engagement off Endau up the eastern Malayan coast from Singapore, on January 26, 1942, K6379 was seen to dive into the sea. It was one of 13 of the torpedo-bombers lost that day.

Further up the eastern coast on February 9, the Vildebeests were flying from a strip at Kuantan and K6385 was destroyed on the ground by Japanese aircraft. By late February 1942 surviving British forces had regrouped in central Java, including two serviceable Vildebeests. On the 29th K6384 failed to return from a recce and it is believed to have been shot down near Semerang, east of Jakarta. With that the big biplane's last stand was over. 🎯

# HANDLEY PAGE
# HEYFORD
## 1934 TO 1941

**Right**
*The prototype Heyford, J9130, making the type's debut at the June 1932 Hendon display. The '12' on its side was a 'New Types Park' number, used to help the audience – and the commentators – to recognise the newcomers. A month later, J9130 was wrecked in an accident at North Coates.*

With its distinctive format, the Heyford always attracted a lot of attention at air displays and open days. It was the RAF's last biplane bomber, but it had many of the attributes of the next generation of monoplanes.

The airframe was all-metal, fabric covered and very sleek-looking, despite being a biplane. The Heyford was very agile, often surprising intercepting fighters with its evasive manoeuvres during exercises.

There was purpose in mounting the lower wing below the fuselage. It allowed an almost unrestricted field of fire for the nose and dorsal gunners. A retractable, manually operated turret was located in the ventral position. This had 'stops' to prevent the gunner training on his own wings, but this position known as the 'dustbin' was intended to cover the vulnerable 'behind and below' aspect.

The centre section of the lower wing was where the bulk of the impressive war load was contained in 'cells' – small bomb bays. Although Handley Page boasted that this meant the bomb racks were in easy reach of armourers, it was back-breaking work to manhandle them below the low-lying centre section and into the cells.

The prototype Heyford – the Mk.I – first flew on June 12, 1930. The first operational examples joined 99 Squadron at Upper Heyford in December 1934, replacing the previous Handley Page bomber, the Hinaidi.

The last operational unit flying

out. Both had a similar wing area: the Hendon 1,446sq ft (134.33m²) and the Heyford 1,470sq ft, and power, each of the Hendon's Rolls-Royce Kestrels was 25hp (18.6kW) more powerful than those on a Heyford III. Both carried almost the same bomb load: the Hendon had a top speed of 155mph (249km/h) while the biplane managed a very respectable 142mph.

Only in range did the Hendon outclass the Heyford: 1,360 miles (2,188km) over the Heyford's 920 miles. The figures that really count

## HANDLEY PAGE HEYFORD IA

| | |
|---|---|
| **Type:** | Four-crew heavy bomber |
| **First flight:** | June 12, 1930, entered service December 1933 |
| **Powerplant:** | Two 575hp (428kW) Rolls-Royce Kestrel IIIS V12 |
| **Dimensions:** | Span 75ft 0in (22.8m), Length 58ft 0in (17.6m) |
| **Weights:** | Empty 9,200lb (4,173kg), All-up 16,900lb (7,665kg) |
| **Range:** | 920 miles (1,480km) |
| **Max speed:** | 142mph (228km/h) at 13,000ft (3,962m) |
| **Armament:** | Three machine guns, one in nose, one in dorsal and one in retractable ventral position. Up to 2,600lb (1,179kg) of bombs in lower wing centre section |
| **Replaced:** | HP Hinaidi, Vickers Virginia, from 1935 |
| **Taken on charge:** | 124 |
| **Replaced by:** | Armstrong Whitworth Whitley, Vickers Wellington, from 1937 |

Heyfords was 166 Squadron at Leconfield. It began working up on Armstrong Whitworth Whitleys in September 1939. Heyfords soldiered on in crew training roles until early 1941.

The final flights were made by K5184, which joined the Royal Aircraft Establishment at Farnborough in July 1940. It was last used for trials, towing General Aircraft Hotspur I assault glider prototypes in April 1941.

## HEYFORD V HENDON
When 38 Squadron received its first Fairey Hendon monoplanes (page 32) at Mildenhall in December 1936, the type was heralded as a major leap in the RAF's capabilities. Analysis of the statistics did not really bear this

are how many were built: just 15 Hendons were completed; Heyford production finished in July 1936 with the last of 124 rolling out of the factory.

## NIGHT TO REMEMBER
In October 1935, Heyford IIs were delivered to the re-formed 102 Squadron at Worthy Down; the unit moving to Finningley in September the following year. In December 1936 the unit sent seven Heyfords to Aldergrove in Northern Ireland for an exercise. On the 12th the bombers took off into the darkness to return to their Yorkshire base. Only Sgt Biddulph arrived at Finningley close to the briefed time.

Over the Pennines the Heyfords

**Left**
*Heyford I K3490
served initially
with 10 Squadron
at Mildenhall from
November 1935.
The retractable,
rearward-firing
ventral turret – known
as the 'dustbin' – is
extended. K3490
ended its days at
West Freugh with 4
Bombing and Gunnery
School in July 1940.*
© ANDY HAY
www.flyingart.co.uk

**Left**
*A Hawker Demon
'intercepting'
Heyford I K3490 of
99 Squadron in late
1934. The closeness
of the attack was for
the benefit of the
photographer.* KEC

**Below**
*Heyfords attended
the annual Hendon air
display en masse for
the first time in 1934.
In the aircraft park to
the left are Boulton
Paul Overstrands and
Gloster Gauntlets,
which would make
this scene 1935 at
the earliest. Close
inspection reveals
six radial engines
on 'stalks' in the
background belonging
to a trio of Saro Cloud
training amphibians.*

encountered severe freezing conditions the Heyford had no de-icing aids – and there was scattered, thick fog. Leading the flight was Sqn Ldr Charles Attwood in K4868. He made a text book forced-landing in a field at Jackson Edge, near Disley, southeast of Manchester.

Attwood was followed in by Plt Off M Clifford in K6898. Unsure of the terrain, Clifford executed a 'go-around', but his undercarriage hit a wire fence, impeding a climb away; the Heyford hit further fences and a telegraph pole and came to a slithering halt.

The following morning, Attwood flew K4868 out of the field and returned to Finningley. There he discovered that Fg Off John Gyll-Murray in K5188 had successfully force-landed near York; he landed at Finningley later in the day. That was four accounted for, what of the others?

Sgt Williams in K4864 encountered fog and brought his Heyford down near Blyborough in Lincolnshire. He and his crew were safe, but the bomber was wrecked. Over

## "A retractable, manually operated turret was located in the ventral position... known as the 'dustbin' – it was intended to cover the vulnerable 'behind and below' aspect."

Lancashire, Flt Lt Charles Villiers was losing control of K4874 due to ice accretion on the wings. He ordered his crew to take to their parachutes. All landed safely while the Heyford impacted near Oldham.

Near Hebden Bridge in Yorkshire, Sgt Otter found K6900 was becoming increasingly uncontrollable. With terrible visibility and unaware of his position, he descended but the aircraft hit high ground. Otter was injured; his crew of three were killed.

At Martlesham Heath, the Aeroplane and Armament Experimental Establishment had been evaluating anti-icing systems. Ironically, in early 1939, Flt Lt A E Clouston flew Heyford III K5184 at Martlesham to test a liquid-based system fitted into 'mats' on the wing leading edges. Clouston concluded that inflatable 'boots', which broke up instead of dissolving ice, were more effective. Wars come and go, but hostile weather is a constant enemy. ◉

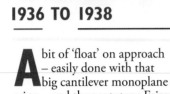

# FAIREY
# HENDON

## 1936 TO 1938

A bit of 'float' on approach – easily done with that big cantilever monoplane wing – and the prototype Fairey Night Bomber overran on landing. Nobody was hurt and the big, all-metal, airframe would repair. Tests up to that point on March 15, 1931 had revealed several shortcomings and the opportunity was taken to include several major changes.

This was a gamble, the prototype Handley Page Heyford had flown for the first time in June 1930 and the lead Fairey had established over its rival was being eroded.

Fairey chief test pilot Norman Macmillan had taken the prototype, K1695, for its maiden flight on November 25, 1930. With him was David Hollis Williams, the bomber's chief designer, acting as observer. No matter how 'safe' a new aircraft might appear, test flying was never without danger. Should something have gone drastically wrong, losing the prototype would have been bad enough, but to be left without its designer and a very experienced pilot might have been catastrophic for Fairey.

From the factory at Hayes in Middlesex, Fairey's products had previously been taken by road to Northolt for test flying. In 1929 the RAF requested the company found somewhere else and land was acquired at Harmondsworth and London's Great West Aerodrome was created. Today, the site is lost within the vast concrete jungle that is Heathrow Airport.

### REBUILD AND RETHINK

In terms of design it was a major departure for Fairey, and turned out to be the largest original design ever built by the company. The Air Ministry was hoping to place three-figure orders for what would be the RAF's first monoplane heavy bomber, so the risk was worth it.

A new factory at Heaton Chapel, Stockport was opened to help with the likely expansion. Maiden flights took place from Manchester's municipal airport, Barton.

The Fairey Night Bomber (it was not until October 1934 that it adopted the name Hendon) set the format of all the monoplane 'heavies' that served with the RAF through World War Two. The fuselage was deep enough for a large bomb bay that could accommodate two of the RAF's latest weapon, the 1,000-pounder.

There were three turrets, manually operated in the Hendon's case, in nose, dorsal and tail positions. The cockpit was off-set to port to allow access to the front gun and the bomb aiming position in the extreme nose.

The rethink of the prototype was comprehensive and costly. The 525hp (391kW) Bristol Jupiter radials were replaced with Rolls-Royce Kestrels. The wing's aerofoil section was changed and rods instead of cables (which stretched) actuated the flying controls. All of this involved major re-engineering work.

A retrograde step removed the original enclosed canopy for the pilot and navigator, replacing it with open cockpits. For the production examples the canopy was reinstated. A handful were finished as dual-control trainers, recognisable by

the stepped-up rear portion of the canopy.

The much-rebuilt prototype took to the air again on November 13, 1931. Despite the changes, evaluation at the Aeroplane and Armament Experimental Establishment at Martlesham Heath favoured the Heyford. The Handley

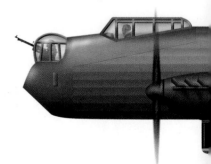

Page biplane won the lion's share of the contracts and 124 were built.

Fairey received a consolation order for 14 Hendons, almost certainly not economically viable, and follow-on orders of 62 were cancelled. The Hendon may have been a dismal financial performer for Fairey, but it pointed the way forward – monoplanes were the future.

## PULLING BACK

Just one unit was destined to fly the Hendon operationally. The first production aircraft, K5085, was delivered to 38 Squadron at Mildenhall on September 24, 1936, before a change of base in May

### FAIREY HENDON II

| Type: | Five-crew heavy bomber |
|---|---|
| First flight: | November 25, 1930, entered service December 1936 |
| Powerplant: | Two 600hp (447kW) Rolls-Royce Kestrel VI V12 |
| Dimensions: | Span 101ft 9in (31.0m), Length 60ft 9in (18.51m) |
| Weights: | Empty 12,773lb (5,793kg), All-up 20,000lb (9,072kg) |
| Max speed: | 155mph (249km/h) at 15,000ft (4,572m) |
| Range: | 1,360 miles (2,188km) |
| Armament: | One machine gun in nose, mid-upper and rear position. Up to 2,660lb (1,206kg) of bombs |
| Replaced: | Handley Page Heyford |
| Taken on charge: | 15 |
| Replaced by: | Vickers Wellington I, from late 1838 |

1937 saw the Hendons settled in at Marham.

The Hendon's story ended more or less as it began – with one of the big bombers 'pancaked' on an airfield. One night in November 1938 a pair of LACs took dual-control K5094 for a jaunt at Marham. As the Hendon lurched into the air, at about 150ft (45m) one of the miscreants 'bottled' and pulled the throttle back.

The Hendon stalled and its fuselage fractured aft of the wing trailing edge as it hit the ground. After their very brief, unauthorised sortie, K5094's two 'crew' suffered only cuts and bruises. Far worse was to come; they were confined while they awaited a court martial.

That same month, 38 Squadron received its first Vickers Wellington Is and the conversion was completed by January 1939. Six Hendons were ferried out of Marham for use as ground instructional airframes by 1 Electrical and Wireless School at Cranwell to help train the next generation of aircrew. ◉

Above left
*A dual-control Hendon, very likely K5092, at Marham in May 1938. This machine was delivered to 38 Squadron in January 1937 and was retired in January 1939.*

Below
*Hendon I K5085 was the first production example, having its maiden flight at Barton on September 24, 1936. It was retired from service with 38 Squadron in January 1939 and became an instructional airframe at Cranwell.*
© ANDY HAY
www.flyingart.co.uk

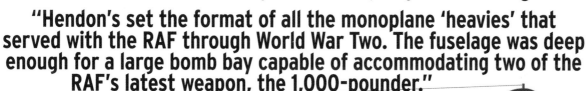

## "Hendon's set the format of all the monoplane 'heavies' that served with the RAF through World War Two. The fuselage was deep enough for a large bomb bay capable of accommodating two of the RAF's latest weapon, the 1,000-pounder."

# ARMSTRONG WHITWORTH
# WHITLEY

## 1937 TO 1943

Z6633

WL G

**Above**
*Whitley VIII Z6633 of 612 Squadron based at Davidstow Moor. It carries the complex aerial array of the Anti-Surface Vessel Mk.II radar. This machine served with 612 from the autumn of 1941 until June 1943.*
PETE WEST

Two months after the prototype Whitley completed its maiden flight, on March 17, 1936, the Air Ministry placed an order for 80 Mk.Is. When the RAF's previous heavy bomber, the Hendon, made its debut in November 1930 it took just over two years to sign a contract and it was for a paltry 14 aircraft. Six years later the world was a very different place, Britain had a lot of catching up to do.

Hitler, having gained absolute power, was re-arming Germany at an alarming pace. Ten days before the first Whitley took to the air, the German army occupied the previously demilitarised Rhineland, and four months later the Spanish Civil War erupted.

In October, Germany and Italy announced the Rome-Berlin Axis, a treaty of mutual co-operation bringing the territorially ambitious Mussolini into Hitler's orbit. Half the world away, Japanese expansionistic intents were becoming obvious.

Britain could be facing three wars, in western Europe, in the Mediterranean and in the Far East. In 1936 the UK announced a rapid expansion of its own armed forces in response to growing world tensions.

Alongside Handley Page Hampdens and Vickers Wellingtons, Whitleys were the first generation of Bomber Command's strike force that might be called on to deter, or failing that, attack, a variety of enemies.

With increased power, armament and equipment changes, Whitley Is, IIs and IIIs were built at the Armstrong Whitworth factory at Whitley – the origin of the bomber's name – and, from late 1936 at the

| ARMSTONG WHITWORTH WHITLEY I | |
|---|---|
| **Type:** | Five-crew medium bomber |
| **First flight:** | March 17, 1936, entered service March 1937 |
| **Powerplant:** | Two 810hp (608kW) Armstrong Siddeley Tiger IX radials |
| **Dimensions:** | Span 84ft 0in (25.6m), Length 69ft 3in (21.1m) |
| **Weights:** | Empty 14,275lb (6,475kg), All-up 21,660lb (9,824kg) |
| **Max speed:** | 135mph (217km/h) at 16,000ft (4,876m) |
| **Range:** | 1,250 miles (2,011km) |
| **Armament:** | Two machine guns in nose turret, two in rear turret. Up to 3,365lb (1,526kg) of bombs |
| **Replaced:** | Handley Pages Heyford, Vickers Virginia from 1937 |
| **Taken on charge:** | 1,814 |
| **Replaced by:** | HP Halifax from 1941, Consolidated Liberator and Vickers Wellington from 1943 |

huge new assembly plant at Baginton, Coventry.

With the Mk.IV the switch was made to the ubiquitous Rolls-Royce Merlin. This engine was also fitted to the Mk.V, the variant produced in the largest numbers (1,466), which appeared in 1939. The final version was the Coastal Command configured GR.VII; the Mk.VI remaining on the drawing board.

The Whitley was inaugurated into the RAF by 10 Squadron at Dishforth, receiving its initial examples in March 1937. Whitleys went into action during the opening night of the war and were the first RAF bombers over Berlin, dropping propaganda leaflets on October 1/2, 1939. The type was withdrawn from the Bomber Command inventory in late 1942.

## SUB-KILLER
Whitleys proved to be reliable workhorses for Coastal Command.

Two incidents in May 1943 over the Bay of Biscay illustrate their typical involvements in the struggle against U-boats in the twilight of the type's frontline career.

Aircrews dreamed of finding U-boats on the surface and just after midnight on May 1 a Wellington XII of Chivenor-based 172 Squadron did just that. Caught in the glare of its searchlight was U-415 on its way back from a patrol and heading for Brest in France.

Gunners on the submarine put up effective defensive fire, but the Wellington unleashed six depth charges (DCs) and damaged its quarry. Slowed down, U-415 continued on its way, but with a 'live' contact and a likely direction, Coastal Command was determined not to let it slip away.

Around midday a Short Sunderland flying-boat of 461 Squadron RAAF engaged U-415, again on the surface.

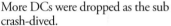

More DCs were dropped as the sub crash-dived.

As the light was failing, U-415 was once more on the surface making as much speed as it could for France. It was the turn of a Whitley VII of 612 Squadron, operating out of Davidstow Moor to have a go. The sub's gunners put up withering fire at the bomber, which let its DCs go wide of the mark. The Whitley came around for another try, this time more accurately. The sub escaped and several days later, it arrived in Brest; its crew having had a horrifying time while Coastal Command stalked it.

On May 13 another Pembroke Dock based Sunderland, this time of 228 Squadron, caught U-564 unawares. The flying-boat inflicted serious

damage on the exposed U-boat, but the sub's gunners shot DV967 down, killing its crew.

The U-boat had been on its way out into the Atlantic to begin a killing spree but had to turn around and limp back to Brest. At St Eval, 10 Operational Training Unit (OTU) had an anti-submarine flight to make the most of the skills of its Whitleys and instructors.

Captaining Mk.V BD220 was Australian Sgt A J 'Buzz' Benson and he was directed to the area where the U-564 was expected to be. He found the submarine on the surface and for two hours faithfully shadowed it, reporting its position.

With armed DCs on board, Benson decided that action was called for

and attacked through a hail of flak from his target. The submarine was straddled and it sank with all hands.

The Whitley had been damaged and it became clear that it would not make landfall in England. After ditching, a French fishing boat picked up the crew and took them to France where they became prisoners of war.

The offensive role of 10 OTU was exceptionally valuable against the U-boats during the campaign from the summer of 1942 until July 1943 when the Whitleys were withdrawn. The intention was to harass U-boats, but pilots like Benson seized opportunities. As the crew of BD220 proved 10 OTU's aggressive sorties were not without loss: 33 of the unit's Whitleys failed to return. ◎

**Above left**
*Close-up of a Nash and Thompson FN4A-powered, four-gun turret on a Whitley IV. The type was the first with this formidable armament.*

**Above**
*Whitley IVs on the production line at Baginton, Coventry.*
KEC

**Below left**
*A Whitley of 51 Squadron on approach to its base at Dishforth. The unit operated Mk.IIs, IIIs, IVs and Vs from February 1938 to November 1942.*

## "Whitleys went into action during the opening night of the war and were the first RAF bombers over Berlin, dropping propaganda leaflets on October 1/2, 1939."

# BRISTOL
# BLENHEIM

## 1937 TO 1944

**Right**
*Blenheim Mk.IV V6083 of Bicester-based 13 Operational Training Unit, 1942. Built by Rootes Securities at Speke, it retired in March 1944.*

Captain Frank Barnwell, chief designer for Bristol, came up with a very clean-looking twin-engined eight-seater with retractable undercarriage that might appeal to businesses and the rich – a 1930s Learjet. Lord Rothermere, patron of the Daily Mail and a great supporter of British aviation, got wind of the Type 142 project and ordered one, which he declared would carry the name *Britain First*.

When it was evaluated in 1935, Rothermere's flagship ruffled feathers. It had a top speed 54mph (87km/h) *faster* than the state-of-the-art Gloster Gladiator biplane fighter that had just been ordered for the RAF. Here was a twin with obvious potential to become a 'heavy' fighter or a bomber.

Point made, his lordship presented *Britain First* to the nation. In August 1935 an appreciative Air Ministry ordered 150 military-configured Type 142Ms. The incredible Blenheim had been conceived.

Our sister publication, *Fighters*, details the Blenheim's role as stop-gap long-range interceptor and pioneer of radar interception. The first production Blenheim I, K7033, took its maiden flight on June 25, 1936.

Introducing the Blenheim into RAF frontline service, and as a bomber, was 114 Squadron at Wyton in March 1937. The type fought in every theatre of World War Two: Europe, North Africa, Greece, the Middle East, India and the Far East.

Blenheim Is were taken off the production lines in late 1938 and the long-nosed Mk.IV became the standard, both in fighter and bomber form. At Odiham, 53 Squadron inaugurated the new version into service in January 1939. Blenheims were withdrawn from Bomber Command in August 1942 but the type continued to give good service in second-line roles into 1944.

## SMOKE SCREEN

During the summer of 1941 Odiham-based 13 Squadron traded in its Westland Lysanders for Blenheim IVs. Exercises with the army were still the order of the day and crews honed their skills in low-level bombing and strafing. The Mk.IVs were also adapted to carry smoke screen generators and canisters for spraying gas. Thankfully the latter were never deployed, but 13 Squadron did get to lay smoke in anger.

### BRISTOL BLENHEIM IV

| | |
|---|---|
| **Type:** | Three-seat light bomber |
| **First flight:** | September 24, 1937; Mk.IV entered service March 1939 |
| **Powerplant:** | One 920hp (686kW) Bristol Mercury XV radials |
| **Dimensions:** | Span 56ft 4in (17.12m), Length 42ft 7in (12.97m) |
| **Weights:** | Empty 9,790lb (4,440kg), All-up 13,500lb (6,123kg) |
| **Max speed:** | 266mph (428km/h) at 12,000ft (3,657m) |
| **Range:** | 1,450 miles (2,333km) |
| **Armament:** | One machine gun in port wing, one in dorsal turret and two in remotely controlled, rearward-firing 'chin' turret. Up to 1,320lb (598kg) of bombs |
| **Replaced:** | Hawker Audax and Hind from 1937; Boulton Paul Overstrand 1938; Hawker Hector, Fairey Battle 1939; Westland Lysander 1941 |
| **Taken on charge:** | 1,134 (all Mk.Is), 3,296 (all Mk.IVs). Production sub-contracted to Avro and Rootes Securities. (Also built in Canada by Fairchild as the Bolingbroke.) |
| **Replaced by:** | Handley Page Halifax and Vickers Wellington from 1940; Boeing Fortress, de Havilland Mosquito and Lockheed Hudson from 1941; Douglas Boston, Lockheed Ventura and Vultee Vengeance from 1942 |

## "While over Dieppe, V5626 of 614 Squadron was hit by what today would be called 'friendly fire', and Flt Lt J Scott turned west, hoping to make landfall in Britain."

For the first of the 'Thousand Bomber' raids, to Cologne on the night of May 30/31, 1942, the Blenheims of 13 Squadron were called to join others in disrupting the Luftwaffe's response. A force of 49 Blenheims was despatched to interdict enemy night-fighters at their bases along the route of the bomber stream.

Two aircraft failed to return, both from 13, with six aircrew killed: N3616, captained by Plt Off R Cundy, was shot down into the North Sea and Z6186, flown by Flt Lt D Redman, was brought down near Venlo airfield in the Netherlands.

The smoke-laying skills were called upon to support Operation 'Jubilee', the gallant, but ill-fated, amphibious in-and-out raid on the French port of Dieppe on August 19, 1942. Blenheims of 13 and 614 Squadrons, along with Douglas Bostons, were tasked with obscuring the landing points from dawn onwards.

Plt Off C Woodland and crew perished when flak hit V5380, while Blenheim IV Z6089, piloted by Flt Lt E Beverley, was damaged by gunfire. It limped back as far as Thruxton airfield, where it force-landed with no casualties – including the Blenheim,

which was repaired.

It became apparent that V5380 had been hit by the Royal Navy amid the chaos of the assault. Worse was to follow.

While over Dieppe, V5626 of 614 Squadron was hit by what today would be called 'friendly fire', and Flt Lt J Scott turned west, hoping to make landfall in Britain. He brought the stricken bomber down at Friston in Sussex but 'hung up' smoke and phosphorous canisters ignited as it slid to a halt.

Flt Sgt G Gifkins had died over the target and Sgt W Johnson succumbed to his wounds on August 21. Unconscious, Scott was pulled from the inferno and recovered – and was awarded a Distinguished Flying Cross for his brave attempt bring his crew to safety.

### DIVE-BOMBER

There was one further Blenheim adaptation, for which the aircraft briefly carried another name. Specification B6/40 called for a twin-engined type for ground attack and dive-bombing. Bristol responded with a modified Blenheim – the first of two prototypes, with the name Bisley, flying on February 24, 1941.

Two versions were initially offered: a day bomber with a glazed nose offset to port, or a strike aircraft with a solid nose toting four machine guns. With more powerful Bristol Mercury radials, armour plate and an effective, but bulky, Bristol B.X two-gun dorsal turret, the bomber version was ordered.

The name Bisley was dropped and the new machine manufactured by Rootes Securities at Blythe Bridge, near Stoke-on-Trent, as the Blenheim V. Production ended in June 1943 by which time 940 had been made: they were the last of the British-built Blenheims.

First to receive the Mk.V was 614 Squadron at Odiham in August 1942, the unit deploying to North Africa the following month. Combat experience revealed the type was slower and less manoeuvrable than previous Blenheims. Without escort, Mk.Vs were vulnerable and poorly regarded by their crews.

By late 1943, Blenheim Vs had been withdrawn from the front line in Italy and in the Far East. In the Persian Gulf, 244 Squadron soldiered on with them on coastal patrols until they were replaced by Wellington XIIIs in April 1944. ◉

**Above**
*Built in 1938, Blenheim I LI311 joined 62 Squadron at Cranfield in 1939. The unit, part of the reinforcements for Singapore, was declared operational at Tengah in September 1939. It ditched off Penang, Malaya, on April 4, 1940.* PETE WEST

**Below**
*Wearing the colours of a 139 Squadron Blenheim IV, the RAF Museum's example is a Fairchild-built Bolingbroke IVT which served the Royal Canadian Air Force as 10001 from October 1942 to May 1946. It became part of the Canadian National Aeronautical Collection before being acquired by the RAF Museum on April 25, 1966.* RAF MUSEUM WWW.rafmuseum.org

# FAIREY
# BATTLE

## 1937 TO 1944

### FAIREY BATTLE

| | |
|---|---|
| Type: | Three-seat light bomber |
| First flight: | March 10, 1936; entered service May 1937 |
| Powerplant: | One 1,030hp (768kW) Rolls-Royce Merlin II V12 |
| Dimensions: | Span 54ft 0in (16.45m), Length 42ft 2in (12.85m) |
| Weights: | Empty 6,647lb (3,015kg); all-up 10,792lb (4,895kg) |
| Max speed: | 241mph (387km/h) at 13,000ft (3,962m) |
| Range: | 795 miles (1,279km) |
| Armament: | One machine gun in starboard wing, another in rear position. Up to 1,000lb (453kg) of bombs |
| Replaced: | Hawker Hart, Hind and Vickers Wellesley from 1937 |
| Taken on charge: | 2,200, including sub-contract to Austin Motors |
| Replaced by: | Bristol Blenheim IV and Handley Page Hampden from 1939, Handley Page Halifax and Vickers Wellington from 1940 |

Many readers will regard the Battle as a dismal failure. It had many limitations, but was the best in its class at the time; there was nothing to put in its place. Branding the aircraft as a disaster is to decry the incredible valour shown by the aircrew that did what they could to face the German Blitzkrieg of May 1940.

The Battle was a modern, monoplane rethink of the incredibly successful Hawker Hart and Hind line of light bombers. But a concept that worked in the late 1920s and early 1930s was eclipsed by the rapidly changing technologies that heralded the start of World War Two.

The prototype took its maiden flight on March 10, 1936 and in May the following year the Battle entered service with 63 Squadron at Upwood.

On September 2, 1939 – the day before war was declared – 226 Squadron became the first Battle unit to deploy to France as part of the Advanced Air Striking Force (AASF) intended to deter any German ambitions to expand westwards.

After the Battle of France and Dunkirk, Battles were quickly replaced and in 1941 the type was withdrawn from operational flying. Battles were adapted to support roles, as pilot conversion and gunnery trainers and target-tugs, and served on until 1944.

### ACT OF FAITH

With just less than twice the power of the Hart, the Battle carried the same defensive armament (single fixed forward-firing gun and a manually operated one in the dorsal position) and twice the bomb load. Yet it was only 57mph (91km/h) faster and, crucially, was more than twice as heavy, fully loaded.

Battles were underpowered, sluggish and pitifully armed – which made them easy meat for the far faster, exceptionally agile Messerschmitt Bf 109s they would encounter on the way to a target – and formed the most numerous bomber element of the AASF: the RAF had slightly more than a thousand on charge in September 1939.

With Hawker Hurricanes heavily committed, the Battles went into combat largely without escort. Despite being well trained and highly motivated, their crews, flying into the teeth of the Luftwaffe, were doing so as an act of faith.

### BLACK TUESDAY

German tanks, artillery and troops, supported by wave after wave of Luftwaffe aircraft, crossed into

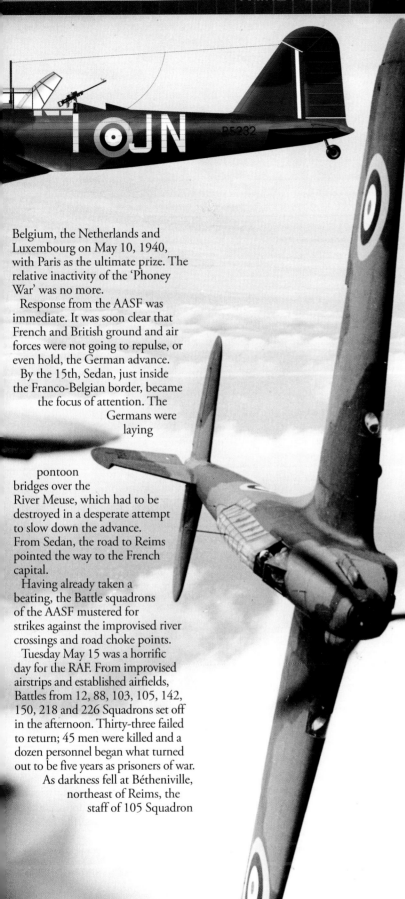

Belgium, the Netherlands and Luxembourg on May 10, 1940, with Paris as the ultimate prize. The relative inactivity of the 'Phoney War' was no more.

Response from the AASF was immediate. It was soon clear that French and British ground and air forces were not going to repulse, or even hold, the German advance.

By the 15th, Sedan, just inside the Franco-Belgian border, became the focus of attention. The Germans were laying pontoon bridges over the River Meuse, which had to be destroyed in a desperate attempt to slow down the advance. From Sedan, the road to Reims pointed the way to the French capital.

Having already taken a beating, the Battle squadrons of the AASF mustered for strikes against the improvised river crossings and road choke points.

Tuesday May 15 was a horrific day for the RAF. From improvised airstrips and established airfields, Battles from 12, 88, 103, 105, 142, 150, 218 and 226 Squadrons set off in the afternoon. Thirty-three failed to return; 45 men were killed and a dozen personnel began what turned out to be five years as prisoners of war.

As darkness fell at Bétheniville, northeast of Reims, the staff of 105 Squadron began to appreciate that their unit had suffered the most: seven aircraft gone, 12 dead and one taken prisoner.

Airborne from Écury-sur-Coole, southeast of Reims, at 15:24 hours, Battle P5232 *I-for-Ink* of 150 Squadron, piloted by Flt Sgt G T Barker with observer Sgt J Williams and gunner LAC A K Sumerson, was shot down and crashed at Raucourt-et-Flaba, south of the Meuse. Barker and Williams were killed. *Ink* was one of four Battles lost by the squadron that day.

Volume 1 of Bill Chorley's masterful *Bomber Command Losses* (Classic 2013) provides proof that not every aspect of war is inhuman. Terribly burned and with an injured leg, Sumerson managed to evade the Germans – all the more remarkable as their direction of travel was the same as his.

After 72 hours he was picked up by French personnel and rushed to a hospital in Verdun. Interned, he was eventually allowed to return to Britain on humanitarian grounds, travelling via Spain and Gibraltar and arriving in the UK in March 1941.

Like most Battle units, 150 Squadron never recovered from the action of May 15. Changing bases twice as the Germans marched relentlessly onwards, the unit evacuated in early June and began regrouping at Abingdon on the 15th. By October it was at Snaith and converting to Vickers Wellingtons. ◉

**Left**
*Battle I K7674 of 12 Squadron cavorting for the camera. Issued to the unit at Andover on February 23, 1938, it retired in February 1940, becoming an instructional airframe.*

**Bottom left**
*On the day German forces broke into the Netherlands, Luxembourg and Belgium, May 10, 1940, the Battles of 12 Squadron operating from Amifontaine in France were detailed to attack troop concentrations in Luxembourg. Canadian Plt Off A W Matthews had to force-land the damaged L5190 in a field near Kirchberg. The crew of three became prisoners of war. German personnel are seen here inspecting the wreckage.*
PETER GREEN COLLECTION

# VICKERS
# WELLESLEY

## 1937 TO 1944

Remembered for its huge wing span and long-range record-breaking flights, the *real* legacy of the Wellesley was much more sweeping, it was truly a game changer. It prepared the way for the incredible Wellington and set Vickers up as a giant of the aviation industry.

While Wellesleys were making awesome non-stop expeditions, early auto-pilots, fuel-management systems and the like were being trialled and evaluated. This work paid dividends as Bomber Command matured into a strategic weapon, hitting deep into Europe.

In the summer of 1931 the Air Ministry issued Specification G4/31 looking for a general purpose, light bombing and torpedo-carrying type to replace Fairey Gordon and Westland Wapiti biplanes. In depression-ridden Britain, the winner of this contract was looking at a lifeline. No fewer than *nine* companies – Armstrong Whitworth, Blackburn, Bristol, Fairey, Handley Page, Hawker, Parnall, Vickers and Westland built prototypes for a fly-off.

Vickers boldly put forward biplane *and* monoplane prototypes for evaluation, both conceived by former airship designer Barnes Neville Wallis. Each employed his pioneering new construction technique – geodetics – offering lighter, stronger and more durable airframes.

The biplane design 'played safe' by using geodetics for the 'shell', but with the backstop of conventional light alloy longerons. The monoplane

employed the new structure throughout.

The biplane G4/31 first flew at Brooklands on August 16, 1934 and went on to win the hard-fought competition. The Air Ministry ordered 150 units.

The monoplane had its maiden flight on June 19, 1935 and it was immediately clear it was a massive leap forward. The Air Ministry re-issued the contract in October 1935 and eventually 176 were delivered. By that time the 'general purpose' nature

of the new aircraft was dropped; the big-span Vickers monoplane had the makings of an interim bomber.

## PAVING THE WAY

On January 30, 1937 the first production Wellesley, K7713, was flown. Three months later 76 Squadron at Finningley became the type's first unit. With a span of 74ft 7in (22.73m) the Wellesley was big – the twin-engined Wellington's wing was only 11ft 5in (3.5m) longer.

Often confused as external fuel

## VICKERS WELLESLEY

| | |
|---|---|
| **Type:** | Two-seat bomber / general purpose |
| **First flight:** | June 19, 1935, entered service April 1937 |
| **Powerplant:** | One 925hp (690kW) Bristol Pegasus XX radial |
| **Dimensions:** | Span 74ft 7in (22.73m), Length 39ft 3in (11.96m) |
| **Weights:** | Empty 6,369lb (2,888kg), All-up 12,500lb (5.670kg) |
| **Max speed:** | 206mph (331km/h) at 20,000ft (6,096m) |
| **Range:** | 1,335 miles (2,148km) |
| **Armament:** | One machine gun, firing through propeller arc, another in rear position. Up to 2,000lb (907kg) of bombs in under-wing panniers |
| **Replaced:** | Fairey Gordon, Hawker Audax, HP Heyford from mid-1937 |
| **Taken on charge:** | 176 |
| **Replaced by:** | Fairey Battle and HP Hampden from 1939 |

tanks, the Wellesley carried a detachable, streamlined pannier under each wing for up to 2,000lb (907kg) of bombs. These were needed because the 'egg shell' nature of the geodetic structure prevented large interruptions – such as bomb bays – an egg is very tough, provided it keeps its shape. By the time Wallis designed the Wellington, also a geodetic airframe, he had overcome this problem.

On June 18, 1937 a Soviet aircraft approached US air space from over the North Pole – two decades later this would be the stuff of Cold War nightmares. With a giant wing spanning 111ft 6in the ANT-25 had been specially created by Andrei Tupolev's design bureau to wave the flag for the USSR. It touched down at Portland in Washington State – an

incredible feat, but Soviet leader Stalin expected better.

Twenty-five days later, the ANT-25 took off from an airfield near Moscow and landed at San Jacinto, California. It had been in the air for 62hrs 17mins and had travelled 7,145 miles (11,498km) to set a new world record.

Perhaps as a direct consequence of this feat, at Upper Heyford a special RAF unit was established on New Year's Day 1939. It was the Long Range Development Unit (LRDU) under the command of Wg Cdr Oswald Gayford DFC AFC. He had flown Fairey Long Range Monoplane K1991 non-stop from Cranwell to Walvis Bay, South Africa, in February 1932, a distance of 5,410 miles.

In the still, cool air of pre-dawn at Ismailia in Egypt on November 5,

1938, three LRDU Wellesleys took off, determined not to land until they reached Australia. One aircraft, low on fuel, had to drop out at Kupang in Timor, but that was still exceptional aviating.

The other two made it all the way to Darwin, Northern Territory, touching down at midday on the 7th after 48 hours in the air. They had flown 7,158 miles, a vitally important 13 miles *more* than the ANT-25!

Setting the record was the overt aim of LRDU, but it had a much more important task, hence the word *Development* in its title. Before it disbanded on January 23, 1939, LRDU had immeasurably improved Bomber Command's knowledge of automated boost and mixture controls, superchargers, flying clothing, navigation techniques, leadless fuel and crucially the behaviour of three-axis auto-pilots. Behind the sensational headlines, LRDU was readying the next generation of bombers for all-out war.

### AFRICAN WARPLANE

There is a myth that by the start of World War Two, the Wellesley was out of service, or relegated to second-line duties. Italy entered the war on June 10, 1940 and conflict immediately erupted in North and East Africa. Wellesleys were in action from the start, bombing the Eritrean port of Massawa.

On August 18 Wellesleys attacked the Abyssinian capital, Addis Ababa. An Italian air strike on the forward base at Gedaref in the Sudan on October 16 caught 47 Squadron unawares and eight Wellesleys were destroyed on the ground.

Last to fly the Wellesley operationally was 47 Squadron, which retired them from coastal patrols off the Libyan coast in March 1943. But the type was still not finished, it was not until July 12, 1944 that the Khormaksar Station Flight in Aden gave up and struck K7726 off charge. Not bad for a big-winged aircraft that was 'only' used for record breaking. ◉

**Left**
*Wellesley L2697 of 14 Squadron, based at Amman, Transjordan, 1938.*
© ANDY HAY WWW.flyingart.co.uk

**Below left**
*Manhandling L2639 of the LRDU at Ismailia, Egypt, prior to the epic flight, November 1938.* KEC

# HANDLEY PAGE
# HAMPDEN

## 1938 TO 1944

Lessons came thick and fast for Bomber Command in the first month of the war, September 1939. Equipped with the Hampden medium bomber, which was almost as fast as the Bristol Blenheim, the crews of 144 Squadron at Hemswell were in confident mood. The mid-morning of September 29 changed all that.

The target was warships in the waters between the island of Heligoland and the Elbe estuary off the northwest German coast. Two flights of six Hampdens set out; one of the first batch had to turn back with engine trouble.

Both elements should have arrived around the same time, entering the target area from the south and the north to ensure separation. The southerly section – with six aircraft – arrived early and attacked two destroyers, but with no visible results.

As this group pulled out, the others arrived at around 10:00 hours. Alerted to the raid, Messerschmitt Bf 109s

were racing to the area, the fighters having climbed out of Jever, west of Bremerhaven, and just 44 miles (70km) away from Heligoland. The navigation couldn't have been easier: the island was due north of the base.

It took less than ten minutes to dispatch all five Hampdens. Fifteen men died in the water, one succumbed to his injuries after being picked up and four became prisoners of war. Among the dead was 144's commanding officer, Wg Cdr J C Cunningham.

German radio was quick to crow about the destruction of an entire flight of British bombers. The broadcast declared that the RAF had "stirred up a hornets' nest" and paid the penalty. It is perhaps as well that the announcer was not aware of 144 Squadron's motto, approved in March 1938: 'Who Shall Stop Us'.

By the end of September, Bomber Command dramatically reduced sorties while its tactics were reassessed. When the Hampdens

returned to operations, their single dorsal and ventral guns had been replaced by twin guns, while armour plating had been introduced in an attempt to make them more resilient. But they remained terribly vulnerable to a frontal attack.

## FLYING SUITCASE

Its deep fuselage tapering abruptly into a tail boom led to the Hampden being nicknamed 'Flying Suitcase' and 'Flying Panhandle' – while the Luftwaffe referred to it as the 'Tadpole'. The origin of its proper name came from townships in Canada or New Zealand; the RAF was coy as to which took the honour.

The Hampden was a combination of simplicity – shunning power-operated turrets – and aerodynamic elegance. It was the fastest of the trio of medium bombers with which the RAF entered the war: 70mph (112km/h) ahead of the Armstrong Whitworth Whitley and 19mph

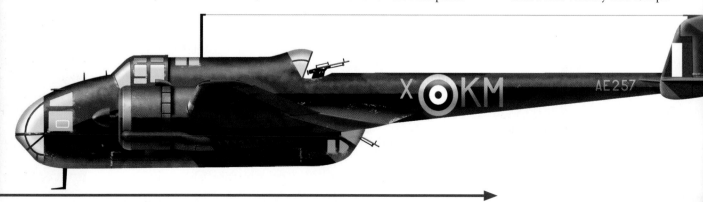

## "Its deep fuselage tapering abruptly into a tail boom led to the Hampden being nicknamed 'Flying Suitcase' and 'Flying Panhandle' – while the Luftwaffe referred to it as the 'Tadpole'."

Lancashire from the beginning of 1940 to allow the parent company to start the Halifax assembly line rolling.

Hampdens were withdrawn from Bomber Command operations by mid-September 1942. Coastal Command employed them as torpedo bombers until the advent of the Bristol Beaufighter in late 1943. By that time, Hampdens were also being supplanted at operational training units (OTUs).

better than the Vickers Wellington. It was only 12mph slower than the lightweight Bristol Blenheim.

Unlike the Whitley and the Wellington, the Hampden had been designed from the start to be constructed in sub-assemblies, enabling the most efficient use of sub-contractors supplying the assembly plants.

The prototype first flew on June 21, 1936 and the type entered frontline service with 49 Squadron at Scampton in August 1938. Production was handed over to English Electric at Samlesbury in

### HANDLEY PAGE HAMPDEN

| | |
|---|---|
| Type: | Four-crew medium bomber |
| First flight: | June 21, 1936; entered service August 1938 |
| Powerplant: | Two 1,000hp (746kW) Bristol Pegasus XVIII radials |
| Dimensions: | Span 69ft 2in (21.08m), Length 53ft 7in (16.33m) |
| Weights: | Empty 11,780lb (5,343kg), all-up 22,250lb (10,092kg) |
| Max speed: | 254mph (408km/h) at 14,000ft (4,267m) |
| Max range: | 1,885 miles (3,033km) |
| Armament: | One fixed machine gun and one free-mounted machine gun in the nose plus two each in dorsal turret and ventral position. Up to 4,000lb (1,814kg) of bombs |
| Replaced: | Avro Anson, Hawker Hind from 1938; Armstrong Whitworth Whitley, Bristol Blenheim, Fairey Battle, Vickers Wellesley from 1939 |
| Taken on charge: | 1,453 (100 Herefords by Shorts, 23 converted to Hampdens); sub-contract to English Electric and Canadian Associated Aircraft |
| Replaced by: | Avro Manchester, Handley Page Halifax from 1941; Vickers Wellington from 1942; Bristol Beaufighter from 1943 |

### DAGGER OPTION

A version of the Hampden powered by the troublesome 24-cylinder, H-format 955hp (712kW) Napier Dagger VIII entered limited production as the Hereford. The prototype, converted from a Hampden, took its maiden flight in October 1938.

The Hereford's disappointing performance and reliability meant only a handful saw service with the Hampden-equipped 185 Squadron at Cottesmore from August 1939 to April 1940. The remainder of the 100 manufactured joined OTUs.

Manufacture of Herefords was entrusted to Short and Harland at Sydenham, Belfast, the first example appearing in May 1939. If nothing else the Dagger-engined variant prepared the workforce to tackle mass production of the Short Stirling 'heavy'. ◎

**Left**
*The dorsal gunner of a Hampden, clad in an Irvin sheepskin-lined leather jacket, showing how exposed his twin Vickers 'K' gun turret was to the elements. The metal bar protruding from the fuselage was a handhold to assist in the climb up from the wing's trailing edge.*

**Above**
*A long-term restoration project at the RAF Museum's Michael Beetham Conservation Centre at Cosford is Hampden TB.I P1344. Operating from bases in Murmansk, in northern Russia, 144 Squadron flew torpedo-equipped Hampdens in September and October 1942 in defence of the Arctic convoys. Shot down on 5th September 1942, the wreckage of P1344 was salvaged in 1990. Illustrated is the centre section showing the dorsal and ventral gun positions. KEN ELLIS*

**Above left**
*The first Short-built Hereford, L6002, at Sydenham around the time of its first flight in May 1939. Note the parallel exhaust stacks of the Napier Dagger H-format engine. KEC*

# VICKERS
# WELLINGTON
## 1938 TO 1954

L4274 KA·K

While the Armstrong Whitworth Whitley and the Handley Page Hampden played an important part in the early stages of World War Two, the Vickers Wellington's contribution to Bomber Command was crucial. The type bore the brunt of the offensive until the four-engined 'heavies' gained momentum.

In the spring of 1941 the Wellington's generous bomb bay enabled it to introduce the 4,000lb (1,814kg) 'Cookie' – or blockbuster – bomb into the RAF's arsenal. The last frontline use of the 'Wimpey', as the Wellington was fondly known, with Bomber Command took place in October 1943,

At that point, its career was far from over, having already carved an important niche with the operational training units, as a bomber in the Middle East and a vessel and sub-killer with Coastal Command.

All of this was made possible because far-sighted Vickers planned it to be mass-produced from the outset. It was not just a case of the ability to churn them out through the factory doors; Wellingtons were robust and repaired relatively easily.

As experience of operations was fed back to the company, alterations were implemented relatively quickly, particularly in defensive armament. Wellingtons adopted by Coastal Command meanwhile sprouted radar aerials, searchlights and, later, radomes with apparent ease.

The airframe was capable of accepting different engines to increase power as weights rose. Bomber versions began with the 1,000hp (746kW) Bristol Pegasus (Mk.I) followed by the Rolls-Royce Merlin X of 1,145hp on the Mk.II and even the 1,200hp Pratt & Whitney Twin Wasp on the Mk.IV.

The ubiquitous Bristol Hercules III of 1,375hp was first used on the Wellington III introduced in 1939.

The first high-flying version, the Mk.V, used supercharged Hercules VIIIs, in late 1940. Rated initially at 1,675hp, the Wellington X and the most sophisticated Coastal Command variants also used 'Hercs'. First appearing in July 1942, the Mk.X reached the highest individual production figure – 3,803.

## ONE-A-DAY

Having designed the R100 airship, Barnes Neville Wallis knew how to make structures that were light yet strong. Sir Robert McLean, the chairman of Vickers, was determined to turn the designer's talents to fixed-wing aircraft: Wallis came up with geodetics, a lightweight 'basket-weave' providing exceptional strength.

The technique formed a robust outer structure that could adopt considerable curvatures – internal fittings etc were added as the airframe progressed down the factory floor.

Tests at Farnborough found that the

BU·R 778

new structure exceeded all previous requirements by a significant margin. The Vickers Wellesley (page 40) was the first RAF type to feature geodetics.

The system made for ease of manufacture and repair. By the time the Wellington was being finalised, Vickers stunned the Air Ministry by announcing in 1937 that, if ordered in hundreds, one bomber could be built every 24 hours.

Trevor Westbrook took on the task of creating the new bomber en masse and worked with Wallis to standardise the geodetic sections so that there were fewer variations – and made them lighter still. By thinking *beyond* the prototype, Vickers made sure the new type would enter service smoothly and quickly. This made the 'one-a-day' claim a far from idle boast.

On June 16, 1936 test pilot 'Mutt' Summers took the prototype

Wellington, K4049, for its maiden flight at Brooklands. Also on board were Wallis and Westbrook; the consequences of a disaster during that first foray do not bear thinking about. Two months later, 180 were ordered, long before the official RAF evaluation.

While being tested by the Aeroplane and Armament Experimental Establishment at Martlesham Heath, the prototype broke up in mid-air on April 19, 1937; the pilot escaped but the flight engineer was killed. It was discovered that when the large horn balance on the elevator was exposed to the airflow at full travel it flipped the aircraft onto its back.

A 'fix' was introduced to the first Mk.I, L4212, which first flew on December 23, 1937 – a remarkably short time after the prototype's first excursion. This aircraft took into account all of the feedback from the Martlesham evaluation and differed in many ways from K4049.

The first operational Wellington was issued to 99 Squadron at Mildenhall in October 1938. Brooklands was already geared up for production and, to stick to the one-a-day promise, two new factories were set up. First on stream was Hawarden, near Chester, which completed its first Mk.I, L7770, in August 1939. A year later the second facility, Squires Gate, Blackpool, carried out the maiden flight of Mk.Ic X3160.

On October 13, 1945 the last-ever Wellington, Mk.X RP590, rolled off the Squires Gate production line. A grand total of 11,460 had been built, far more than any other British bomber. Wellingtons retired from RAF service, as T.10 crew trainers, in 1954, bringing to an end an astounding career. ◎

## VICKERS WELLINGTON IC

| Type: | Six-crew heavy bomber |
|---|---|
| First flight: | June 15, 1936, entered service October 1938 |
| Powerplant: | Two 1,000hp (746kW) Bristol Pegasus XVIII radials |
| Dimensions: | Span 86ft 2in (26.26m); length 64ft 7in (19.68m) |
| Weights: | Empty 18,556lb (8,417kg); all-up 28,500lb (12,927kg) |
| Max speed: | 235mph (378km/h) at 15,500ft (4,724m) |
| Range: | 2,550 miles (4,103km) |
| Armament: | Two machine guns each in nose and tail turrets; one machine gun in port and starboard beam positions. Up to 4,500lb (2,041kg) of bombs |
| Replaced: | Fairey Hendon and Handley Page Heyford from 1938; Handley Page Harrow from 1939; Bristol Blenheim and Fairey Battle from 1940 |
| Taken on charge: | 11,460 |
| Replaced by: | Short Stirling from 1941; Avro Lancaster and Handley Page Halifax from 1942; Consolidated Liberator from 1943 |

**Above left**
*Wellington III X3763 of 425 Squadron RCAF. As 'L-for-Love' it was shot down on an 'op' to Stuttgart out of Dishforth on April 15, 1943; all six crew were killed.*

**Left**
*Currently undergoing a major restoration at the Michael Beetham Conservation Centre at Cosford, the RAF Museum's Wellington T.10 MF628 as it appeared at Abingdon in June 1968 for the RAF's 50th anniversary celebrations.* KEC

# BRISTOL
# BEAUFORT

## 1939 TO 1946

**Right**
*Pratt & Whitney Twin Wasp-powered, Australian-built Beaufort VIII A9-201 of 100 Squadron, RAAF. Note the machine gun-toting 'Donald Duck' and ducklings nose-art.*
PETER GREEN COLLECTION

## RUNNING THE GAUNTLET

The battle cruiser *Gneisenau* slipped out of dry dock at Brest, France, on April 5 and Coastal Command wasted no time in seizing the opportunity. At 04:20 hours the following morning six Beauforts – three with torpedoes,

Responding to an Air Ministry requirement for a torpedo-bomber and another for a general reconnaissance bomber, Bristol used the rugged Blenheim airframe as a starting point. The two specifications were combined into one and the resultant Beaufort featured a lengthened and deepened fuselage, including a bomb bay.

Two 1,130hp (842kW) Bristol Taurus radials replaced the 840hp Bristol Mercuries, as the Beaufort was a much heavier beast. The prototype first flew on October 15, 1938. Development problems – dominated by the troublesome Taurus – delayed the type's introduction to service until November 1939 when Beauforts ousted the Vickers Vildebeest biplanes of 22 Squadron at Thorney Island.

The 'blood line' had further to go. By mating the Beaufort's wings, tail surfaces and undercarriage to an all-new slim-line fuselage, with robust and reliable Bristol Hercules radials, the incredible Beaufighter was born in July 1939.

Searches for a better engine for the Beaufort settled on another dependable radial, the Pratt & Whitney Twin Wasp. The first Mk.II appeared in November 1940 and the Beaufort became a stalwart of Coastal Command operations although it dropped far more mines and conventional bombs than it did its intended weapon, the torpedo.

Vildebeests were replaced by Beauforts at Seletar, Singapore, when 100 Squadron took the new type in

| BRISTOL BEAUFORT I | |
|---|---|
| **Type:** | Four crew torpedo/reconnaissance bomber |
| **First flight:** | October 15, 1938, entered service November 1939 |
| **Powerplant:** | Two 1,065hp (794kW) Bristol Taurus II |
| **Dimensions:** | Span 57ft 10in (17.37m), Length 44ft 2in (13.46m) |
| **Weights:** | Empty 11,839lb (5,370kg), All-up 20,000lb (9,072kg) |
| **Max speed:** | 265mph (426km/h) at 6,000ft (1,828m) |
| **Range:** | 1,510 miles (2,430km) |
| **Armament:** | One fixed machine gun in the port wing, one free-mounted machine gun in the nose, two in dorsal turret. One 1,548lb (702lb) 18in (45cm) torpedo or up to 2,200lb (997kg) of ordnance |
| **Replaced:** | Vickers Vildebeest from 1939, Avro Anson from 1940, Bristol Blenheim from 1941, Vickers Wellesley 1942 |
| **Taken on charge:** | 1,429, plus 700 built under licence in Australia |
| **Replaced by:** | Lockheed Hudson from 1941, Consolidated Liberator and Handley Page Hampden from 1942, Bristol Beaufighter from 1943 |

November 1941. With the Japanese invasion, the remnants retreated to Java before the unit disbanded in February 1942. Australia built Beauforts under licence and the Royal Australian Air Force used them to great effect in New Guinea from 1942.

Beauforts were withdrawn from British-based frontline units in August 1942. They remained in operational use in the Mediterranean and Ceylon until September 1944.

With its capacious fuselage the Beaufort was ideal as a crew trainer, particularly in the instruction of the demanding art of dropping torpedoes. The last examples of the breed were retired in autumn 1946.

three carrying mines – of 22 Squadron took off from St Eval for a co-ordinated attack.

Only Fg Off Ken Campbell in N1016 *X-for-X-ray* managed to fight through atrocious weather and arrive on time. He and his crew pressed home the attack alone and succeeded in blowing a 40ft (12m) hole in the side of the ship and over 3,000 tons of water flooded in.

The warship was condemned to return to its dry dock. It did not venture out again until the 'Channel Dash' of February 11, 1942 when the *Gneisenau*, *Prinz Eugen* and *Scharnhorst* slipped through the English Channel and into the North Sea.

Only one other Beaufort from 22 Squadron found Brest, half an hour after Campbell's strike. By then, the harbour defences were on full alert – the pilot sought cloud and returned to base.

Campbell and his crew, Canadian Sgt J P Scott, Sgt W C Mullis and F/Sgt R W Hillman, did not survive the onslaught from the harbour's defences. They are buried at a local cemetery.

Campbell was awarded the Victoria Cross and the *London Gazette* of March 13, 1942 described how he was: "...detailed to attack an enemy battle cruiser in Brest Harbour at first light...

"The ship was in a position protected by a stone mole bending round it, and rising ground behind on which stood batteries of guns. Other batteries clustered thickly round the two arms of land which encircled the outer harbour, while three heavily armed anti-aircraft ships moored nearby guarded the cruiser.

"Even if an aircraft penetrated these formidable defences it would be almost impossible, after attacking at low level, to avoid crashing into the rising ground beyond. Knowing all this, Fg Off Campbell ran the gauntlet of the defences and launched a torpedo at point-blank range, severely damaging the battle cruiser below the water-line, so that she was obliged to return to the dock she had left only the day before.

"By pressing home the attack at close quarters in the face of withering fire, on a course fraught with extreme peril, this officer displayed valour of the highest order."

**Above left**
Fg Off Ken Campbell's Beaufort I N1016 of 22 Squadron spring 1941. It is carrying an 18in torpedo.
© ANDY HAY
www.flyingart.co.uk

**Left**
The RAAF Museum's Beaufort is an amalgam of the remains of three ex-RAAF Australian-built Mk.VIIIs salvaged from Tadji, Papua New Guinea, and handed over in 1991. To the right is a Leigh retractable searchlight, as fitted to Coastal Command Wellingtons.
RAF MUSEUM
www.rafmuseum.org

**Below left**
Beaufort I L9878, built in 1940, served 217 Squadron at St Eval until it was retired in the spring of 1943.

# AVRO MANCHESTER

## 1940 TO 1943

**Right**
*Repair work is carried out on L7477 of 61 Squadron at Woolfox Lodge. The Manchester had taken part in Operation 'Fuller', the 'Channel Dash' of February 12, 1942 – see page 46 – and had been peppered by flak from the German fleet. KEC*

"Accept from me personally, and on behalf of my command and my service, salutations upon the signal honour, so well merited, which His Majesty the King has seen fit to confer upon your gallant son. No Victoria Cross has been more gallantly earned.

"I cannot offer you and yours condolence in personal loss in circumstances wherein your son's death and the manner of his passing must so far surmount, by reason of the great services he rendered to his country and the last service to his crew, all considerations of personal grief.

"His shining example of unsurpassed courage and staunchness to death will remain an inspiration to his service and to his unperishable memorial."

So ran a handwritten letter dated October 23, 1942 to the Manser family of Radlett, Hertfordshire, and signed simply Arthur T Harris.

Plt Off Leslie T Manser and the crew of Manchester L7301 *D-for-Don* of 106 Conversion Flight – but on loan to 50 Squadron at Skellingthorpe – had failed to return from the first 'Thousand Bomber' raid, to Cologne, on the night of May 30/31, 1942.

A force of 45 Manchesters had been despatched from Balderton, Coningsby, Scampton, Skellingthorpe, Syerston and Waddington. Manser's L7301 was one of four lost, with 13 aircrew perishing.

It was late October when Harris put pen to paper; yet he was writing about an event in May. Bomber Command was not that far behind with its administration – as summer turned to autumn five of *D-for-Don*'s crew, who had managed to evade capture, gave testified to their skipper's valour.

Over the target, L7301 was mauled by flak and came down as low as 700ft (213m) before Manser pulled the stricken machine back into a climb to about 2,000ft. They set course for home, but the port engine failed and its propeller was feathered.

Manser knew the bomber was doomed and, in its single engine state, he'd need to stay at the controls to

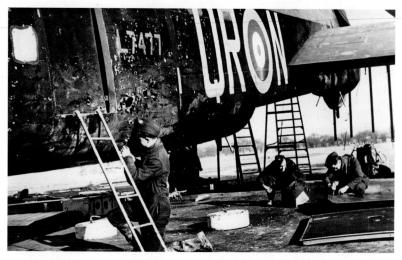

give the others a chance of getting out of a stable aircraft. He gave the order to bale out and Plt Offs R Barnes, R Horsley and Sgts E Finch, S King and A Mills took to the silk.

Sgt Leslie Baveystock, a second pilot under tuition who had shut down the recalcitrant Vulture engine, joined Manser to help him put his parachute on. Manser would have none of it, yelling: "For God's sake, get out! We're going down!"

Baveystock baled out and moments later *D-for-Don* keeled over and plunged into the ground. Only Barnes was picked up by the Germans, becoming a prisoner of war. The others managed a 'home run' and, at the debriefing, Manser's selflessness was stressed and recommendations made.

## RIGHT AIRCRAFT, WRONG ENGINE

Both the Halifax and the Lancaster were conceived as twin-engined bombers. Thankfully, the Halifax avoided that stage; its days as a twin were confined to the drawing boards. Not so the Manchester: it was saddled with the hugely complex 24-cylinder, 90° X-format 1,760hp (1,312kW) Rolls-Royce (RR) Vulture.

This engine was essentially two RR Peregrines – as fitted to the Westland Whirlwind fighter – one above the other on a single crankcase. The idea

of such a brutish engine was that it gave the new 'heavies' all the power they needed while allowing stocks of RR Merlins to go exclusively to fighters.

The Air Ministry soon relented, but not before metal was being cut on the two prototype Manchesters. Avro and Metropolitan-Vickers had tooled up the production lines in readiness.

Experience with Armstrong Whitworth Whitleys, Handley Page Hampdens and Vickers Wellingtons had shown that only in the most experienced hands could one of these types with an engine out be brought home. The asymmetric loads on a heavy twin would be virtually impossible – as Manser proved. Production of Merlins showed no signs of waning and the industrial capacity was ready for the new generation of bombers.

The prototype Manchester, L7246, first flew on July 25, 1939 and gave a vivid foretaste of life with the Vulture. It force-landed three times: in Staffordshire on November 29, 1939 on delivery to the Aeroplane and Armament

## AVRO MANCHESTER

| | |
|---|---|
| **Type:** | Seven-crew heavy bomber |
| **First flight:** | July 25, 1939; entered service November 1940 |
| **Powerplant:** | One 1,760hp (1,312kW) Rolls-Royce Vulture 24-cylinder X-format |
| **Dimensions:** | Span 90ft 1in (27.45m); length 68ft 10in (20.98m) |
| **Weights:** | Empty 45,000lb (20,412kg); all-up 56,100lb (25,446kg) |
| **Max speed:** | 284mph (457km/h) at 17,200ft (5,242m) |
| **Range:** | 1,630 miles (2,623km) |
| **Armament:** | Nose, mid-upper and tail turrets with two, two and four machine guns respectively. Up to 10,250lb (4,449kg) of bombs |
| **Replaced:** | Handley Page Hampden from 1940 |
| **Taken on charge:** | 200, including sub-contract to Metropolitan-Vickers |
| **Replaced by:** | Avro Lancaster from 1942 |

# "The Manchester was saddled with the hugely complex 24-cylinder, 90° X-format 1,760hp Rolls-Royce Vulture."

Experimental Establishment at Boscombe Down; and twice in the circuit at Boscombe, on December 12 and 23.

After 200 Manchesters, the production lines were to switch, almost seamlessly, to what was briefly designated the Manchester III –

the Lancaster. The comparatively small fleet went on to incredible achievements in the face of considerable mechanical problems, let alone what the weather and the Third Reich threw at them.

Picking up its first Manchesters at Boscombe Down, 207 Squadron settled in to Waddington in November 1940 to begin the task of converting to the Manchester. Not long after Operation 'Millennium', the 'Thousand Bomber' attack on Cologne of late May 1942, the type withdrew from the front line.

Pressures on Bomber Command were such that the retired Manchesters were not sent to the scrapheap but used for crew training until the middle of 1943. As will be seen on page 56, the Lancaster proved that Roy Chadwick's design was a world-beater if given the right engines. ◎

# SHORT STIRLING

## 1940 TO 1946

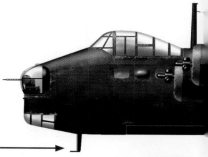

Veteran test pilot John Lankester Parker sat in the prototype Short Stirling, L7600, at Rochester, ready for take-off on May 14, 1939. This was his 32nd maiden flight since May 1918. Alongside him was co-pilot Sqn Ldr Eric Moreton, on loan from the RAF. George Cotton acted as observer and 'wheel-winder' should the electrical system fail and the massive, stalky undercarriage need to be brought up – or put down – manually.

The 20-minute debut went well; the Stirling had good characteristics. But as L7600 touched down the big machine spun around, the undercarriage crumpled and collapsed. Nobody was hurt and it was discovered that a brake had seized.

It was December 3 before Parker ventured skywards in the second example, L7605. Prior to his retirement, Parker carried out two more first flights, of the prototype G-Class and Shetland flying-boats.

The undercarriage plagued the Stirling throughout its career. Why was it so tall and so complex? Destined to be the first four-engined 'heavy' to enter RAF service, the Short design staff, under Arthur Gouge, found that expediency governed most decisions.

Originally the Stirling was to adopt the 112ft 9in (34.36m) wing structure of the Sunderland flying-boat but the Air Ministry insisted on a span of less that 100ft. The wing was redesigned, increasing the broad chord profile and stunting the bomber's operating height.

Until the advent of the Stirling, Short had no experience of a retractable undercarriage. Gouge opted for multiple oleos instead of a simpler and more robust forged casting. The latter would have cost time and money in an already tight development schedule.

The first Stirlings were issued to 7 Squadron at Leeming in August 1940. With the introduction of the Halifax and Lancaster raid planners were faced with complications because the Stirling could not fly as high as either of these, requiring careful attention

## SHORT STIRLING III

| Type: | Seven/eight crew heavy bomber |
|---|---|
| First flight: | May 14, 1939, Mk.I entered service August 1940 |
| Powerplant: | Four 1,650hp (1,230kW) Bristol Hercules XVI radials |
| Dimensions: | Span 99ft 1in (30.20m), Length 87ft 3in (26.59m) |
| Weights: | Empty 43,200lb (19,595kg), All-up 70,000lb (31,752kg) |
| Max speed: | 270mph (434km/h) at 14,500ft (4,419m) |
| Range: | 2,010 miles (3,234km) |
| Armament: | Nose, mid-upper and rear turrets with two, two and four machine guns respectively. Up to 14,000lb (6,350kg) of bombs |
| Replaced: | Handley Page Hampden from 1940, Vickers Wellington from 1941, Boeing Fortress from 1942 |
| Taken on charge: | 2,368 including sub-contract to Austin Motors |
| Replaced by: | Avro Lancaster from 1943, Handley Page Halifax from 1944 |

to target approaches. By mid-1943 Stirlings began to be phased out and the type flew its last raid with Bomber Command in September 1944.

Stirlings found new use as glider tugs and dropping supplies on 'special duties' sorties. The Mk.IV was converted to exclusive transport roles and the final version, the Mk.V was built from scratch as a turret-less transport. In this guise the final Stirlings were withdrawn from RAF service in March 1946.

## FAMILY TRAGEDY

Newly delivered to 15 Squadron at Wyton, Stirling I N6086 *F-for-Freddie* had been carefully bedecked with two family crests and the name *MacRobert's Reply* just below the cockpit. The bomber was the centrepiece of a bitter-sweet naming ceremony on October 10, 1941.

American-born Lady Rachel Markham MacRobert had donated £25,000 to finance N6086. In present-day values that figure would approximate to £1,375,000, but it is perhaps best put in context by knowing the average annual wage in Britain for 1940 was £248.

The reason for the gift was prompted by tragedy. Eldest son and heir Alasdair had died in a civilian flying accident on June 1, 1938.

Middle son Flt Lt Roderic

MacRobert was posted to Habbaniya in Iraq. Flying a Hawker Hurricane, 26-year-old Roderic was killed while raiding Mosul airfield on May 16, 1941. It is thought he was hit by fragments from a Messerschmitt Bf 110 he had bombed at ultra-low level.

On the last day of June 1941, Plt Off Iain MacRobert, 24, took off from Thornaby flying Blenheim IV Z5982 of 608 Squadron on an air-sea rescue sortie. Ian and his crew of three were not seen again.

The MacRobert dynasty was no more. Hence the purchase of N6086, Lady MacRobert noted that through the Stirling, her sons: "would be glad that their mother replied for them and helped to strike a blow at the enemy."

## MACROBERT'S REPLY

Sqn Ldr Peter Boggis captained *MacRobert's Reply* on its first 'op', to Nuremburg, Germany, on October 12, 1941. Boggis commanded N6086 on at least five more occasions, including an attack on the Skoda factory at Pilsen in Czechoslovakia on the 28th from which *Freddie* returned with flak damage to the rear fuselage.

A daylight sortie on December 18 in N6086 was the last 'op' Boggis flew with 15 Squadron. The destination was the harbour at Brest, France, and on the home leg one of the gunners shot down a Bf 109.

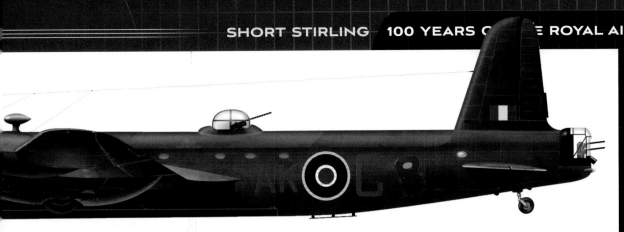

# "Lady MacRobert noted that through the Stirling her sons: 'would be glad that their mother replied for them and helped to strike a blow at the enemy.'"

In late January 1942 the squadron was detached to Lossiemouth for operations against the warship *Tirpitz*, moored near Trondheim in Norway. On the 29th N6086 was one of seven Stirlings crossing the North Sea, but all were forced to turn back.

On February 7 the Stirlings set off for Wyton in poor weather. A couple got no further than Peterhead and settled in for the night. The following morning N6086 swung on take-off and slammed into a Spitfire, killing the fighter's pilot.

*MacRobert's Reply* was a broken and twisted hulk, but all of its crew extricated themselves. Before hitching a ride south, groundcrew cut the family badges off the nose so they could be attached to another Stirling.

The crests were riveted to the nose of Austin Motors-built Mk.I W7531 and the wording *MacRobert's Reply* was painted below them. This Stirling was picked because it was *F-for-Freddie* and 15 Squadron was keen to keep to the same individual letter.

*Freddie* lifted off from Wyton with a load of mines, bound for the Danish coast on May 17, 1943. Hit by flak, *MacRobert's Reply* lost an engine and

flew into a withering barrage of fire, crashing in a forest near Galsklint in Denmark. Eight men died, but gunner Sgt D Jeffs was thrown clear and became a prisoner of war.

Four Hawker Hurricanes were also purchased by Lady MacRobert during the war. *MacRobert's Reply* was revived in August 1980 when 15 Squadron Hawker Siddeley Buccaneer S.2 XT287 *F-for-Foxtrot* was so named at Lossiemouth by retired Sqn Ldr Peter Boggis DFC.

From 1983 swing-wing Panavia Tornado became 15 Squadron's equipment. By the time 15 disbanded on March 31, 2017, the last Tornado to carry the name *MacRobert's Reply* had been dispatched to Leeming to be reduced to spares: a great pity, it deserved a better fate. 🎯

**Top**
*Stirling III EF252 of 1657 Conversion Unit, Shepherds Grove. This was destroyed when an engine failed on take-off on July 26, 1944; the bomber swung and demolished the Shepherds Grove watch office.* PETE WEST

**Above**
*Sqn Ldr Peter Boggis and a crew member giving a 'thumbs up' from the cockpit of N6086; probably at the hand-over at Wyton, October 10, 1941.* KEC

**Above left**
*Stirling cockpit.*

**Left**
*Stirling Is of 15 Squadron at Wyton, circa 1941.*

1918 2018

# HANDLEY PAGE
# HALIFAX

## 1939 TO 1952

*Right*
*London Aircraft*
*Production Group-*
*built Halifax II Series I*
*BB324 of 10 Squadron*
*performing for the*
*cameras in early 1943.*
*It carries a small*
*cartoon of a terrier*
*wearing a sailor's cap*
*and the name 'Wings*
*for Victory' under*
*the canopy. Based at*
*Melbourne, Yorkshire,*
*BB324 went missing*
*on a raid to Mülheim,*
*Germany, on June*
*23, 1943. All seven of*
*its crew were killed,*
*believed victims of a*
*night-fighter.*

As the Hawker Hurricane was to the Supermarine Spitfire, so it was that the Halifax spent its time in the shadow of the Avro Lancaster. In bombing operations, Lancasters flew nearly twice as many sorties and dropped just under three times as much tonnage as their Handley Page stablemate. But the Halifax had a glittering career that encompassed strategic bombing to the end of the war; action over the high seas with Coastal Command, demanding countermeasures work with 100 Group, hazardous flying on clandestine 'special duties', glider towing, paratroop and supply dropping, transport and training.

It is as well to remind readers that space restrictions mean that the heritage of the RAF's World War Two bombers can only be dipped into. To chart the diversity and valour of Halifax ops here is an impossibility.

Like the Avro Manchester (page 48) the Halifax was conceived as a heavy twin, powered by Rolls-Royce Vulture engines. Thankfully Handley Page avoided the traumas of having to re-engineer its design (Avro morphed the Manchester into the Lancaster) and the prototype initially flew with Rolls-Royce Merlins on October 25, 1939. The first production examples went to 35 Squadron at Linton-on-Ouse in December.

Despite a series of 'rolling' modifications, Merlin-engined Halifaxes had disappointing performance. This was corrected with the Bristol Hercules-engined Mk.III which entered frontline service in October 1943. The Hercules radial transformed the prospects of the Halifax and the type remained in production until November 1946.

During the summer of 1945, Bomber Command withdrew the Halifax from its order of battle. The type remained in use in the transport and airborne forces role into the late 1940s. Coastal Command soldiered on with meteorological reconnaissance Halifaxes until March 17, 1952 when 224 Squadron flew the last 'met' sortie from Gibraltar.

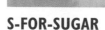

## S-FOR-SUGAR

Half past eight, the evening of April 27, 1942 at Kinloss, 35 Squadron Halifax II W1048 *S-for-Sugar* took off en route for Fættenfjord, near Trondheim, Norway. Target: the 42,000-ton Bismarck-class battleship *Tirpitz*. Crew: Plt Off Don P MacIntyre (pilot); Sgt Vic C Stevens (flight eng); Plt Off Ian Hewitt (nav/bomb aimer); Sgt Dave L Perry (wireless op/air gunner); Sgt Pierre G Blanchett RCAF (mid-upper gunner); Sgt Ron H D Wilson (tail gunner).

Part of a force of 31 Halifaxes and 12 Lancasters despatched from Lossiemouth and Kinloss, *S-for-Sugar* was the eighth into the attack, over the target at 00:30 hours. Canadian-born MacIntyre dropped to 200ft (60m) to deliver his quartet of 1,000-pounder spherical mines and was engaged by heavy anti-aircraft defences. As the weapons were released, W1048's starboard wing burst into flames.

Too low to convert speed into height and try for Sweden, McIntyre put *S-for-Sugar* down on the frozen surface of Lake Hocklingen, east of Trondheim. It was a brilliant bit of flying, Stevens broke his ankle, but all stumbled away from the wreck. With his injury, Stevens became a prisoner of war, the rest of the crew evaded and in 72 hours walked to Sweden.

Built by English Electric at Samlesbury in Lancashire, W1048 had been on charge with 35 Squadron 18 days and had a total flying time of 13 hours 'on the clock'. Before April 28 was out, the ice gave way and the Halifax sank to the bottom, 92ft down.

*Sugar* was one of five bombers lost that night: two Halifax IIs from 10 Squadron, another from 35 and a Lancaster I from 97 Squadron. Including MacIntyre's crew, eight men evaded, ten became prisoners of war and 15 were killed. *Tirpitz* was finally sunk by Lancasters of 9 and 617 Squadrons on November 12, 1944.

## RESURRECTION

In 1971 local divers found *Sugar* and the following September a team from the RAF Sub-Aqua Club carried out a series of dives. The bomber was missing its starboard outer Rolls-Royce Merlin XX, the area where it had taken the most damage from the flak batteries.

Lake Hocklingen was fresh water and the state of preservation was excellent. At the time it was the only substantially intact Halifax in the world.

By using new techniques, such as pneumatic airbags, a recovery for the RAF Museum was very 'do-able'.

**Left**
*English Electric-built Halifax II Series Ia DT580 of 51 Squadron, based at Snaith, late 1942.*
PETE WEST

## HANDLEY PAGE HALIFAX VI

| | |
|---|---|
| **Type:** | Seven-crew heavy bomber |
| **First flight:** | October 25, 1939, Mk.I entered service November 1940 |
| **Powerplant:** | Four 1,800hp (1,342kW) Bristol Hercules 100 radials |
| **Dimensions:** | Span 104ft 2in (31.74m), Length 71ft 7in (21.81m) |
| **Weights:** | Empty 39,000lb (17,690kg), All-up 65,000lb (29,484kg) |
| **Max speed:** | 309mph (497km/h) at 19,500ft (5,943m) |
| **Range:** | 1,260 miles (2,027km) |
| **Armament:** | One machine gun in the nose position, four-gun turrets in mid-upper and tail positions. Up to 12,000lb (5,443kg) of bombs |
| **Replaced:** | Armstrong Whitworth Whitley from 1941, Vickers Wellington from 1942, Armstrong Whitworth Albemarle from 1944 |
| **Taken on charge:** | 6,176, including sub-contracts by English Electric, Fairey, London Aircraft Production Group and Rootes Securities |
| **Replaced by:** | (All roles) Avro Lancaster and Consolidated Liberator from 1943; Short Stirling from 1944; de Havilland Mosquito and Douglas Dakota from 1945 |

With only a few snags, *Sugar* rose to the surface on June 30, 1973 and was towed to the shore.

On August 25, 1973, a Royal Corps of Transport landing craft docked at Ipswich and the bomber was moved by road to the RAF Museum's storage facility at Henlow.

Initially it was intended to fully restore W1048 but after a re-assessment it was decided to display it as though it were resting on the lakebed in Norway. *S-for-Sugar* was brought to Hendon in 1982 and laid out accordingly.

Yorkshire Air Museum at Elvington is home to *Friday the 13th*, an incredible recreation of a Halifax, based on many original or appropriate, elements. That amazing project was completed and unveiled in 1996.

In the previous year, *S-for-Sugar* stopped being the only intact surviving Halifax when a Canadian team succeeded in bringing former 644 Squadron special duties Mk.VII NA337 out of the waters of Lake Mjøsa in Norway. The Halifax had been dropping supplies to partisans when it force-landed in the lake on April 13, 1945. It is displayed at Trenton, Ontario, as proud testament to Canadian bomber crews. ◉

**Top**
*The RAF Museum's Halifax W1048 'S-for-Sugar' on its 'lake bed' at Hendon. It is profiled in the narrative.*
RAF MUSEUM
www.rafmuseum.org

**Left**
*Crowded Tarrant Rushton during the D-Day operation with Airspeed Horsa and General Aircraft Hamilcar assault gliders ready for towing to the beachhead. The Halifaxes are Mk.Vs of 298 and 644 Squadrons; at the head of the line-up is Rootes-built LL402 'F-for-Freddie' of 644 Squadron.* KEC

# MARTIN
# MARYLAND A

## 1940 TO 1946

There were high hopes for the Model 167W attack bomber within the Glenn L Martin Company of Baltimore, Maryland. The United States Army Air Corps wasn't impressed but the French government, desperate to re-arm, ordered 215 examples. Speed was of the essence and Martin invested heavily in a large production line.

Deliveries began in October 1939 and were still taking place as France surrendered to the German blitzkrieg on June 22, 1940. The RAF absorbed the order and named the new bomber after the state in which it was manufactured, Maryland. Throughout the type's brief career many called the slim-line twin the 'Glenn Martin'.

In total 305 Marylands were taken on charge, 155 Mk.Is and 150 of the more powerful Mk.IIs. Many were transferred to the South African Air Force, but the RAF put them to work in North Africa and Malta. It was on Malta that the Maryland rose to fame. The resident 431 Flight was the first unit to use the twin operationally, from September 1939.

Marylands were phased out of RAF service in 1942, mostly in favour of its more developed brother, the Maryland. The only British-based operator was 544 Squadron at Benson which used them for photo-reconnaissance. This was almost certainly the last RAF unit to fly Marylands in a frontline role.

## STUFF OF LEGEND
In the summer of 1940 Flt Lt Adrian 'Warby' Warburton joined 431 Flight at Luqa, Malta. The small unit was tasked to provide reconnaissance of the North African coast and particularly Sicily and southern Italy.

Among the rag-tag of types on charge was a handful of Marylands. The gifted 22-year-old Warburton found the American twin ideal for the purpose; it had relatively good unladen range (1,800 miles [2,896km]), was quite agile (top speed 278mph [447km/h]) and had the punch of four machine guns in the wings.

So began a career in reconnaissance that became the stuff of legend. On October 30 Warburton used the Maryland's guns to good effect, shooting down an Italian Cant Z.506B Airone tri-motor floatplane. Three days later Warburton was on the receiving end; hit by an Italian bullet he slumped unconscious. Navigator, Sgt Frank Bastard, seized the controls, until his pilot recovered sufficiently to return to base.

On November 10 Warburton's Maryland was flying over the Italian naval port of Taranto, in the 'heel' of Italy, and was amazed at how many capital ships were at anchor. The following morning he returned to the harbour, but the cameras weren't functioning. Warburton flew the Maryland so low that his observer claimed to be able to read the names off the bows of the ships!

That evening the famous Taranto raid took place, leaving the Italian fleet in tatters. Warburton was back on the 20th for a post-strike assessment. Typically, he went in close again; returning to Luqa with a radio aerial wire from an Italian warship wrapped around the Maryland's tailwheel.

In the tense and crowded Maltese skies, Warburton was the victim of 'friendly fire'. His Maryland, AR735, was attacked erroneously by a Hurricane while returning to Luqa on February 13, 1942. The Martin was written off while crash landing, but all on board were unharmed.

The work of 431 Flight was such that it was re-formed as 69 Squadron on October 1, 1941. By that time the Marylands were being supplanted by Bristol Beaufighters, Hawker Hurricanes and Supermarine Spitfire IVs.

Warburton, by then a flight lieutenant, was awarded a DFC on February 11, 1941, the first of an impressive array of medals. The citation read: "This officer has carried out numerous long-distance reconnaissance flights and has taken part in night air combats. In October 1940 he destroyed an aircraft [the Z.506] and again, in December,

# D BALTIMORE

## MARTIN BALTIMORE III

| Type: | Four-crew light bomber |
|---|---|
| First flight: | June 14, 1941, entered service January 1942 |
| Powerplant: | Two 1,660hp (1,238kW) Wright Double Cyclone GR-2600 radials |
| Dimensions: | Span 61ft 4in (18.69m), Length 48ft 6in (14.78m) |
| Weights: | Empty 15,200lb (6,894kg), All-up 23,000lb (10,432kg) |
| Max speed: | 302mph (486km/h) at 11,000ft (3,352m) |
| Range: | 950 miles (1,528km) |
| Armament: | Two machine guns in each wing, two in dorsal turret and two in ventral position. Up to 2,000lb (907kg) of bombs |
| Replaced: | Bristol Blenheim from 1942; Lockheed Ventura from 1944 |
| Taken on charge: | 1,575 |
| Replaced by: | Consolidated Liberator, de Havilland Mosquito, Douglas Boston and Vickers Wellington from 1944 |

equipped Mk.IIIs, IVs and Vs.

The first unit to take the Baltimore to war was 223 Squadron at Tmimi, Libya, in January 1942. Australian and RAF Baltimores operated extensively in North Africa, across to Sicily and throughout the Italian campaign.

Under Wg Cdr H N Garbert, 500 Squadron took delivery of its

**Above**
*A Baltimore, believed to be from 454 Squadron Royal Australian Air Force, being man-handled out of the mud on a southern Italian airstrip, 1944.*

**"A Baltimore failed to return from a sortie out of Casenatico in late April 1945. Flying south of Graz in Austria there was a tussle with an ill-informed Soviet fighter and a forced landing was called for."**

he shot down an enemy bomber in flames. Fg Off Warburton has at all times displayed a fine sense of devotion to duty."

Detached to the USAAF's 7th Photographic Reconnaissance Group, Sqn Ldr Warburton DSO* DFC** and US DFC failed to return on April 12, 1944. His body was found in the wreckage of his Lockheed F-5B (modified P-38 Lightning) in 2002 to the west of Munich; it seems he had been shot down.

### UNSUNG BOMBER
By the time the RAF was accepting diverted Marylands from the

French order, the deep pockets of the British Purchasing Commission had already signed a contract with Martin for a much more developed version of the Model 167. This was named Baltimore and it became a reliable, if unsung, bomber used almost exclusively in North Africa and across the Mediterranean.

The Maryland was fitted with 1,200hp (895kW) Pratt & Whitney Twin Wasps, but the Baltimore adopted 1,660hp Wright Double Cyclones. It featured a much deeper fuselage, allowing for a large bomb bay. The more basic Mk.Is and IIs were followed by the turret-

first Baltimores at Pescara on Italy's Adriatic coast in September 1944. Atrocious weather conditions turned Pescara and other airstrips in the region into mud baths and it was not until December that the unit could begin offensive sorties. German troop concentrations, road and rail choke points were the main targets for 500's Baltimores.

The squadron also undertook leaflet dropping and sorties across the Adriatic to Yugoslavia. There the bombers were directed to objectives by partisan forces and 500 also carried out supply drops to the freedom fighters.

A Baltimore failed to return from a sortie out of Casenatico in late April 1945. Flying south of Graz in Austria there was a tussle with an ill-informed Soviet fighter and a forced landing was called for. The crew returned to the unit in the first days of May. By that time 500 Squadron was based at Villaorba and preparing to celebrate VE-Day.

In October 1945 orders were issued to redeploy to Eastleigh in Kenya. There 500 Squadron was re-numbered 249 Squadron. This unit was the last to fly Baltimores, trading them in during the spring of 1946 for de Havilland Mosquitos. ◉

**Left**
*Maryland I AR735 served with 431 Flight and 69 Squadron from Luqa, Malta, from late 1940. It was in this aircraft that Flt Lt Adrian Warburton and his crew were attacked erroneously by a Hurricane while approaching Malta on February 13, 1942.*
PETER GREEN COLLECTION

# AVRO
# LANCASTER

## 1941 TO 1956

Ten Victoria Crosses, 156,000 'ops', 608,000 tons of bombs dropped, the Augsburg diesel plant strike, the Dams raids, toppling *Tirpitz*, 12,000lb (5,443kg) 'Tallboys' and 22,000lb 'Grand Slams' – the valour, the sorties and the stats of the Lancaster's contribution to the heritage of the RAF could fill this special publication. So, apologies, these pages can only skim the surface.

The story of the Lancaster begins with the Manchester, see page 48. The troublesome Rolls-Royce Vultures doomed the twin-engined Avro bomber to extinction. The simplest solution to the shortfall this would create was to switch the Avro and Metropolitan-Vickers production lines to build Halifaxes. Thankfully Avro asserted that a four-engined Manchester was the best option and could be integrated into the factories with speed.

Originally designated Manchester III, the prototype Lancaster (BT308) had its maiden flight on January 9, 1941. Four months later the second example took to the air and the first production machine – L7527, see below – flew five months after that.

This was an incredible achievement, and 44 Squadron at Waddington took the initial frontline bombers by the end of 1941.

Other than the Mk.II versions, the Lancaster stayed loyal to the Merlin, either British or US-built, and the engine's development followed a policy of careful refinement. Instantly recognisable with their 1,650hp (1,230kW) Bristol Hercules VI radials, Armstrong Whitworth manufactured 300 Mk.IIs as an 'insurance' should supply of Merlins be interrupted.

The last Lancaster came off the production line in February 1946 but the type had another three years of service with Bomber Command ahead of it. The type was readily adapted to maritime patrol and it was in this guise that the exceptional Lancaster was paid off, by Coastal Command, in 1956.

### FIRST WARRIOR

The first production Lancaster, L7527, was test flown at Woodford on October 31, 1941. It was initially used for trials by Avro and at Boscombe Down.

It was next issued to 1654 Conversion Unit at Wigsley and used to hone crews for operational

| AVRO LANCASTER I | |
|---|---|
| **Type:** | Seven/eight-crew heavy bomber |
| **First flight:** | January 9, 1941, entered service December 1941 |
| **Powerplant:** | Four 1,640hp (1,223kW) Rolls-Royce Merlin 20 V12s |
| **Dimensions:** | Span 102ft 0in (31.08m), Length 69ft 6in (21.18m) |
| **Weights:** | Empty 36,900lb (16,737kg), All-up 68,000lb (30,844kg) |
| **Max speed:** | 287mph (461km/h) at 11,500ft (3,505m) |
| **Range:** | 1,660 miles (2,671km) |
| **Armament:** | Nose, mid-upper and rear turrets with two, two and four machine guns respectively. Up to 14,000lb (6,350kg) of bombs |
| **Replaced:** | Handley Pages Hampden from 1941, Avro Manchester, Handley Page Halifax from 1942, and Vickers Wellington from 1942, Short Stirling from 1943 |
| **Taken on charge:** | 7,377, including sub-contracts to Armstrong-Whitworth, Austin Motors, Metropolitan-Vickers, Vickers-Armstrongs and in Canada |
| **Replaced by:** | Avro Lincoln from 1945 |

squadrons. An accident in May 1943 put it out of action and after repair it was stored.

On March 3, 1944 L7527 went to war, albeit briefly, when it joined 15 Squadron at Mildenhall. Twenty-three days later, Plt Off T Marsh, skippered L7527 to Essen in Germany. The Lancaster is believed to have exploded near Aachen; all seven crew perished.

With much of its time spent in development flying, L7257 had a much longer life than most Lancasters, clocking just over 353 hours.

## FROM CHASTISE TO GUZZLE

The 22 Lancaster IIIs converted to carry the 'bouncing bomb' – code-named 'Upkeep' – were given the designation Avro Type 464 Provisioning. The term

'Provisioning' was designed to make a very special modification sound remarkably mundane.

Wg Cdr Guy Gibson DSO* DFC* was selected to head a unit at Scampton for special duties: 617 Squadron was formed on March 23, 1943. 'Provisioning' Mk.III ED932 *G-for-George* was issued to 617 on April 30 and it was this machine that Gibson captained during Operation 'Chastise', the breaching of the Möhne and Eder dams on May 16/17.

After the raid, ED932 was recoded as *V-for-Victor* and on February 7, 1945 it was retired. In August 1946, it was brought out of storage for use in Operation 'Guzzle', the disposal of the remaining stocks of Upkeep weapons in the North Sea.

Dropping these by any aircraft not equipped with the special cradle in the bomb bay would have been very difficult.

While taking part in Guzzle, ED932 suffered an accident at Scampton on November 8, 1946. Damage was assessed as Category Ac; repair was possible on site, but was beyond the means of resident units. The aircraft that led Bomber Command's most famous exploit, its captain being awarded a Victoria Cross, was casually struck off charge on July 29, 1947 and scrapped.

## LAST OF BREED

In the *FlyPast* special that celebrated the 75th anniversary of the Lancaster's first bombing raid, on March 3, 1942, Andrew Thomas revealed that the last operational use of the venerable bomber took

place in the Middle East in 1953.

The camera-equipped Lancaster PR.1s of 683 Squadron were based at Habbaniya in central Iraq by May 1952. As well as map-making for the Ordnance Survey (OS), intelligence-gathering flights were also staged in the increasingly unstable region. Much of the work of the RAF in the Middle East at the time was peacekeeping and 'flying the flag' and 683's large silver Lancasters made for an impressive visual presence.

With much of the OS task completed, 683 was scheduled for disbandment at the end of July 1952. For some years Saudi Arabia had cast covetous eyes on the oasis at Buraimi in Oman that was thought to have oil reserves. At the end of August 1952, a Saudi party occupied the area

and refused to withdraw.

With the Lancaster's lengthy endurance and the experience of 683's crews, the unit was considered ideal for patrols over the featureless desert. So instead of disbanding, two aircraft were detached to Sharjah. Operational blockade patrols continued until early November when the task was handed on to the Avro Anson C.19s of 1417 Flight.

The 683 Squadron detachment returned to Habbaniya on November 13, 1953 and the unit disbanded on the 30th. It had fallen to 683 Squadron to bring to an end the Lancaster's illustrious frontline career.

Air Marshal Sir Brian Reynolds, Air Officer Commander-in-Chief

of Coastal Command, presided over an emotional ceremony at St Mawgan on October 15, 1956. Fifteen days previously, the last RAF unit to fly the Lancaster, 1 Maritime Reconnaissance School, better known by its original name, the School of Maritime Reconnaissance (SMR), had disbanded. Sufficient Avro Shackletons were becoming available to take over the training of patrol crews.

The October 15 gathering marked the end of the Lancaster's service with the RAF which had begun with 44 Squadron in December 1941. Only one of the breed, Armstrong Whitworth-built GR.3 RF325, was on hand at St Mawgan but it made a spirited display before heading off for the scrap heap. ◉

# BOEING FORTRESS

## 1941 TO 1946

Much was expected of the new American bomber and the press was invited in strength to see the Boeing Fortress Is of 90 Squadron in the first days of July 1941. The crews were paraded wearing oxygen masks to emphasise that the RAF was wielding a high-flying weapon to strike at the heart of the Third Reich.

The US-based British Purchasing Commission had been seduced by the potential of Boeing's bomber, which had first flown in July 1935. An order was placed for 20 Mk.Is, the equivalent of the B-17C. Having a range in excess of 3,000 miles (4,827km) with a light weapon load, it could cruise at 30,000ft (9,144m) above and beyond the reach of Messerschmitts and the famous Norden sight – claimed that it could put a bomb in a pickle barrel from 10,000ft – the Fortress offered great promise.

Eight hours and 26mins after lifting off from Gander in Newfoundland, Fortress I AN521 touched down at Ayr, Scotland, on April 14, 1941 – the RAF's long-range era had begun. Re-formed on May 7 at Watton, 90 Squadron was tasked to evaluate the Fortress under combat conditions. Its first examples, AN529 and AN534, arrived on May 11 and the unit transferred to its operational base, Polebrook, on June 28.

By then doubts were already setting in. Up for an air test out of West Raynham on June 22, AN522, *J-for-Johnnie* broke up in cloud over Yorkshire; killing its crew. While running up at Polebrook on July 3, *B-for-Beer*, AN528, caught fire and was burnt out. Turbulent conditions over Northamptonshire on July 28 caused AN534, *E-for-Edward* to break up in mid-air.

### BAPTISM OF FIRE

On July 8, 1941 Wilhelmshaven on the northwest German coast was 90 Squadron's first 'op' with the new bombers. Three were dispatched and two of them successfully hit

## "...we would start our Window drop and head for a target, drop token markers and bombs and then head back into France behind the Mandrel screen."

the harbour area. The Fortresses flew at 30,000ft in daylight, and as individuals not in formation, unlike other Bomber Command sorties.

Four B-17s were launched from Polebrook on August 16, two bound for Düsseldorf and two for Brest in France. At 32,000ft over Brest, Plt Off Sturmey and his crew were amazed to be relentlessly engaged by Bf 109s. Three of the crew were killed and another severely injured during the onslaught. Sturmey coaxed AN523, *D-for-Don* in the direction of England and executed a forced landing at Roborough, writing off the bomber in the process.

Another four were sent off to Norway, to strike at the warship *Admiral Scheer,* moored near Oslo on September 8. Only one returned intact. Two, AN525 and AN533 fell to the guns of the Bf 109Fs of Jagdgeschwader 77 at 25,000ft – all 14 on board the two bombers perished. *O-for-Orange*, AN535 limped across the North Sea and crash landed at Kinloss. The crew got out, but the Fortress was beyond repair.

After that, 90 Squadron's Fortresses

were removed from Bomber Command's order of battle. Out of 51 individual sorties, 21 had been scrubbed for one reason or another. Four of the survivors were deployed to Egypt where some raids on North African targets were staged. Subsequently, the Mk.Is joined 220 Squadron at Nutts Corner where the Coastal Command unit appreciated their long range.

Complaints about the Fortresses were legion. Crews, guns and equipment froze at the Boeing's operating altitudes. Coming down from those heights left them vulnerable, all of the gun positions were single, manual and exposed to the slipstream and a rearward attack could not be countered. The Norden bomb sights proved to be both cantankerous and complex.

The Americans were incredulous that the RAF was using B-17s for offensive operations. They were used to constantly developing aircraft in the light of experience – 'work in progress' –and dismissed the B-17C as being fit "only for crew training". By then the USAAF was flying the much improved B-17D, and in January

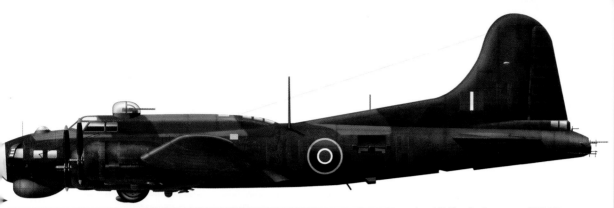

(or ABC) which jammed VHF transmissions, and the electronic device 'Mandrel' and air-dropped reflective foil strips known as 'Window', both of which played havoc with enemy early warning radars.

Established in January 1944 at Sculthorpe, later moving to Oulton, 214 Squadron flew with specially modified Fortress IIs and IIIs. The unit was part of 100 Group in the 'bomber support' role, although this

1942 took delivery of the first of the considerably redesigned and heavily armed E-models.

The tactic of flying aircraft individually also astounded USAAF pilots. Tight formations, giving one another protective fire was the way they went to war.

## SPOOFING

The long endurance of the Fortress made it an ideal platform for Coastal Command, and radar-cquipped Fortress IIs and IIIs entered service from July 1942 when 220 Squadron, by then at Ballykelly, began to replace

its original Mk.Is. The Fortress II was based upon the B-17E and the 'F, while the Mk.III was a version of the most-produced version of the Fortress, the B-17G.

The Fortress was retired from service with Coastal Command in February 1946 when the meteorological reconnaissance 521 Squadron stood down its Mk.IIIs at Chivenor.

Generous space within the fuselage on the Fortress allowed for the carriage of specialist crew and an incredible amount of radio and radar countermeasures gear. Among the apparatus was 'Airborne Cigar'

was widely referred to as 'spoofing'. In August 1944 the Consolidated Liberators IVs of 223 Squadron also settled in at Oulton and began re-equipping with a mixture of Fortress IIs and IIIs in April 1945. Their job done, both units were disbanded in July.

The highly secret nature of the work of 214 and 223 Squadrons was revealed in Laurie Brettingham's book *Even When the Sparrows are Walking* (Gopher, 2001). Canadian Sqn Ldr Mervyn Utas gave an insight into Fortress 'ops': "Sometimes our spoof force would do a double penetration if the Main Force wasn't operating.

"After clearing the Mandrel screen, we would start our Window drop and head for a target, drop token markers and bombs, and then head back into France behind the Mandrel screen. We would then descend to low altitude, orbit for 30 to 45 minutes, then climb back up again and head back into Germany for a second spoof." ◉

## BOEING FORTRESS I

| Type: | Ten-crew heavy bomber |
|---|---|
| First flight: | July 28, 1935, entered service May 1941 |
| Powerplant: | Four 1,200hp (895kW) Wright Cyclone R-1820 radials |
| Dimensions: | Span 103ft 9⸸in (31.63m), Length 67ft 10⸸in (20.68m) |
| Weights: | Empty 31,150lb (14,129kg), All-up 45,470lb (20,625kg) |
| Max speed: | 320mph (514km/h) at 20,000ft (6,096m) |
| Range: | 3,160 miles (5,085km) |
| Armament: | One machine gun in the nose, two each in dorsal and ventral positions, one in each port and starboard beam positions. Up to 4,400lb (1,995kg) of bombs |
| Replaced: | All variants - Bristol Blenheim and Lockheed Hudson from 1941 |
| Taken on charge: | All variants - 184 |
| Replaced by: | Consolidated Liberator from 1943 |

# CONSOLIDATED
# LIBERATOR
## 1941 TO 1946

Five years after Boeing's designers began to detail what became the B-17 Flying Fortress, in the spring of 1939 the Consolidated Vultee team sat down in San Diego, California, to conceive the B-24 Liberator. Such was the pace of progress in aerodynamics, structures and systems that it was effectively a generation ahead of the B-17 and a much more sophisticated aircraft.

In a similar manner to the relationship between the Hurricane and the Spitfire, and the Halifax and Lancaster, it was the Fortress – not the Liberator – that seemed to get all the limelight in the American press. Yet US air and ground crew thought very highly of the B-24, and its war record was exceptional and extremely varied.

The RAF's experience was quite the reverse. As can be seen on page 58, the Fortress had a dismal start to its British service and, although it went on to steadfast service with Coastal Command and 100 Group, it was eclipsed by its comrade from San Diego.

More than 2,000 Liberators served over the hostile waters of the Atlantic in maritime patrol and transport roles, the type also being the RAF's heavy bomber of choice in the Mediterranean, Middle East and South East Asia Command (SEAC).

The Liberator's introduction to the RAF came via an order for 120 LB-30 models from France. Most of these were absorbed by the service, with some used to establish a regular passenger and mail link across the Atlantic – see below. Transport versions of the Liberator remained in operation with the RAF until

August 1946 when the last Mk.IXs were withdrawn at Poona (now Pune) in India.

The first Liberators to join Coastal Command were Mk.Is at Nutts Corner, Northern Ireland, in June 1941. Equipped with increasingly capable anti-surface vessel radar, they continued to patrol the Atlantic convoys from Britain, the Azores and Iceland until specially modified Avro Lancaster GR.IIIs took over in late 1946.

Liberator IIs were the first long-range bomber variant, with Nutts Corner again the debut venue, this time for 160 Squadron in May 1942 – and Liberator VIs of 99 and 356 Squadrons, based on the Cocos Islands in the Indian Ocean, southwest of Java, carried out the last RAF bombing raid of World War Two, on August 7, 1945, the day after an atomic bomb was dropped on Hiroshima.

## ATLANTIC SHUTTLE

Large American-supplied aircraft such as Liberators, Fortresses and Lockheed Hudsons were flown across the Atlantic while smaller types, such as fighters, came by boat. The Atlantic Ferry Organisation was established at Dorval, Montreal, Canada, in November 1940 and run by Canadian Pacific Air Lines. Pilots came from the RAF, British Overseas Airways Corporation (BOAC) and from among commercially rated freelancers.

By their very nature the flights were mostly one-way, eastbound to the ferry terminal at Prestwick in Scotland. Bringing pilots back to repeat the process was

originally a haphazard arrangement, many facing a painfully slow, and risky, voyage dodging U-boats.

In March 1941 the Return Ferry Service (RFS) began, equipped with French-ordered LB-30s. Crews came from BOAC and the RAF, with the first round trip being flown on May 4, 1941.

As well as ferry pilots, the flights carried military and diplomatic personnel along with mail and high-priority freight. At first, the rear fuselages of the LB-30s offered no creature comforts other than mattresses and blankets for a slightly more comfortable seat than the hard, freezing cold airframe.

'Catering' was limited to vacuum flasks of coffee or soup, sandwiches and small 'nips' of rum. With no rationing in Canada, the sandwiches had more nutritious fillings on eastbound flights; westbound, 'Spam' processed meat predominated.

RAF Ferry Command formed on April 20, 1941 to administer the RFS and to better arrange for aircrew to be

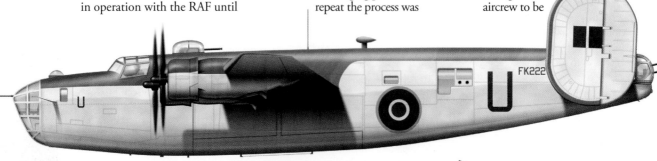

assigned to the duty. From September 1941 till the end of the war, BOAC operated the hard-working Liberators while Scottish Aviation at Prestwick modified and maintained them.

## BRAND LOYALTY

Several RAF units operated Liberators for their entire existence: for example,

### CONSOLIDATED LIBERATOR VI

| | |
|---|---|
| **Type:** | Eight-crew heavy bomber/anti-submarine patroller |
| **First flight:** | December 29, 1939; Mk.I entered service June 1941 |
| **Powerplant:** | Four 1,200hp (895kW) Pratt & Whitney Twin Wasp radials |
| **Dimensions:** | Span 110ft 0in (33.52m), Length 67ft 1in (20.44m) |
| **Weights:** | Empty 37,000lb (16,783kg); all-up 65,000lb (29,484kg) |
| **Max speed:** | 270mph (434km/h) at 20,000ft (6,096m) |
| **Range:** | 2,100 miles (640m) |
| **Armament:** | Two machine guns each in nose, mid-upper and tail turrets. One machine gun in ventral position and one in port and starboard beam positions. Up to 8,800lb (3,991kg) of ordnance |
| **Replaced:** | Vickers Wellington from 1941, Bristol Beaufort and Lockheed Hudson from 1942, Armstrong Whitworth Whitley from 1943, Boeing Fortress and Martin Baltimore from 1944 |
| **Taken on charge:** | 2,181 - all variants |
| **Replaced by:** | Avro York from 1943, Douglas Dakota from 1945, Avro Lancaster from 1946 |

354, 355 and 356 Squadrons serving within SEAC from 1943 to 1945.

One of the most bizarre units of World War One, 159 Squadron formed on June 1, 1918 only to de disbanded 34 days later. Records of its base, if any, are lost in the mists of time and it doesn't appear to have had any aircraft allocated. It's thought it was intended to bolster Royal Flying Corps strength on the Western Front, but was destined to remain a 'paper' squadron.

Reincarnated on January 2, 1942 at Molesworth with Liberator II bombers, 159 Squadron began to work up on the new type, pilots finding the novel tricycle

undercarriage challenging. From then until the unit disbanded in India in June 1946, Liberators were its exclusive equipment – taking on a mixture of Mk.IIIs and Vs in August 1943, Mk.VIs from March 1944 and Mk.VIIIs from June 1945.

The Liberators departed Molesworth bound for Fayid, Egypt, in April 1942 before settling upon Acre and the Aqir in Palestine, from where they flew bombing raids along the North African coast and across the Mediterranean to Greece and southern Italy.

In September, 159 Squadron was on the move eastwards again, arriving at Salbani (present-day Solbani) in

Bengal, eastern India. Flying mostly from this location the unit conducted bombing and mining operations as its main task, but also carried out air-sea rescue searches, support of Special Operations Executive missions and meteorological reconnaissance.

The Liberators flew attacks as far as Siam (Thailand), Indo-China (Vietnam) and the Dutch East Indies (Indonesia), and in October 1944 mined the harbour at Penang, Malaya, blocking it for several days. Such long-ranging sorties involved trips of 3,000-plus miles (4,827km) and 12 hours airborne.

During the afternoon of October 6, 1944, two Liberators of 159 departed Salbani and crossed the Bay of Bengal, bound for a target along the infamous Burma-Siam railway. Both failed to return and 17 aircrew were missing. Squadron personnel received some cold comfort 38 days later when a signal arrived confirming that Fg Off R J Hockings RAAF, F/Sgt R Derrick and Sgt T W Rutter RCAF, part of the crew of Liberator VI BZ992 *E-for-Easy*, were alive and in a Japanese prisoner of war camp. ◎

# DE HAVILLAND
# MOSQUITO
### B

## 1941 TO 1963

When the Panavia consortium was established in 1969, it announced the swing-wing Multi-Role Combat Aircraft (MRCA) programme. This took on the name Tornado in 1974 and the strike version is featured on page 92. Among the press corps at the launch were some who remembered the *original* MRCA, conceived in great secrecy during 1940.

The de Havilland Mosquito was a remarkable aircraft that mastered the roles of fighter-bomber, night-fighter, intruder, bomber and photo-reconnaissance. The concept was to create an aircraft so fast that it did not need defensive armament, and could be built quickly and relatively simply. The inspiration was the DH.4 high-speed bomber of World War One - see page 6.

In his autobiography *Sky Fever* (Hamish Hamilton, 1961) Sir Geoffrey de Havilland CBE described the rationale: "We were confident that this formula would be as novel and as vitally needed as it had been before and that, provided we did not permit orthodoxy especially in the shape of officialdom to stifle us, we could do better still the second time. Our scheme was to discard every item of equipment that was not essential, design for a two-man crew and *no* rear armament, relying on high speed for defence. [It was] estimated that a year

### DE HAVILLAND MOSQUITO IV

| | |
|---|---|
| **Type:** | Two-seat light bomber |
| **First flight:** | November 25, 1940, entered service November 1941 |
| **Powerplant:** | Two 1,250hp (932kW) Rolls-Royce Merlin 21 V12s |
| **Dimensions:** | Span 54ft 2in (16.50m), Length 40ft 9in (12.42m) |
| **Weights:** | Empty 14,600lb (6,662kg), All-up 20,870lb (9,466kg) |
| **Max speed:** | 380mph (611km/h) at 17,000ft (5,181m) |
| **Range:** | 2,040 miles (3,282km) |
| **Armament:** | Up to 2,000lb (907kg) of 'conventional' bombs or a single 4,000lb 'Cookie' bomb |
| **Replaced:** | Bristol Blenheim from 1941, Vickers Wellington from 1942, Bristol Beaufighter from 1943, North American Mitchell from 1945 |
| **Taken on charge:** | 6,439 of all variants in Britain, 7,781 including overseas production. Sub-contracts by Airspeed, Percival, Standard Motors. Also by de Havilland Aircraft in Australia and Canada |
| **Replaced by:** | Handley Page Halifax from 1943, de Havilland Vampire and Venom from 1951, English Electric Canberra from 1952 |

could be saved in production due to the simplicity of wood construction as compared to metal". He concluded: "All this gave us a wonderful opportunity to make an outstanding war aeroplane in almost record time."

Sir Geoffrey's 30-year-old son, Geoffrey, piloted the prototype on its maiden flight at Hatfield on November 25, 1940. It had been designed and built in just 11 months at Salisbury Hall, London Colney. Today, that machine, W4050, is back

at its birthplace, as the centre piece of the de Havilland Aircraft Museum.

The fighter, fighter-bomber and photo-reconnaissance Mosquitos are covered in the sister publication, *RAF Centenary Celebration Fighters*. The initial bomber version was the Mk.IV, the prototype having its maiden flight on September 8, 1941.

From the start the Mk.IV exceeded expectations, its large bomb bay could accommodate four 500lb (226kg) and later even more destructive power

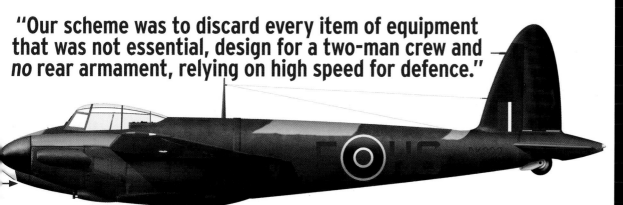

"Our scheme was to discard every item of equipment that was not essential, design for a two-man crew and *no* rear armament, relying on high speed for defence."

was possible - see below. At Swanton Morley, in November 1941 much was made in the press of the first operational Mk.IVs of 105 Squadron.

On May 31, 1942 the unit embarked at dawn on the first of the type's many famous raids, a quartet flying to Cologne in Germany in the immediate aftermath of the 'Thousand Bomber Raid' in order to disrupt rescue and salvage operations. Three of the fast-flying machines returned, but Plt Offs Kennard and Johnson were killed when W4064 was hit by flak.

The Pathfinder Force was formed in August 1942 and Mosquitos were its main equipment. The twins had the endurance and agility to spearhead the heavy bomber streams and mark the targets. From December 1943 the Mk.XVI was introduced and it facilitated another Mosquito-dominated operation, the Light Night Striking Force (LNSF).

Just as the inaugural raid by 105 Squadron emphasised the 'nuisance' factor, the Mk.XVIs and later B.35s of the LNSF were intended to create mayhem finding targets of opportunity and over-loading the German air defence system.

The Mosquito B.35 was paid off by Bomber Command by 1952 with the advent of another multi-role twin-engined wonder, the English Electric Canberra. By this time surplus

B.35s were getting into their stride as target-tugs, a role that was to give the Mosquito a further decade of service. The final TT.35s retired in May 1963.

## VITAL WEATHER EYE

Weather reconnaissance sorties were a vital element of all forms of operational planning and this task mostly fell to Coastal Command during World War Two. At Bircham Newton weather specialist 521 Squadron had been flying a mixture of Mosquito IVs, Bristol Blenheims, Gloster Gladiators, Lockheed Hudsons and Supermarine Spitfire Vs from Bircham Newton. The unit was disbanded on March 31, 1943.

The following day two specialised units came into being to take over 521's duties: 1401 Flight at Bircham Newton to handle North Sea weather data, and 1409 Flight. Based Oakington and later Wyton, adjacent to most Pathfinder units, 1409's Mosquitos undertook sorties deep into Europe bringing back accurate data to provide the raid planners of both Bomber Command and the USAAF Eighth Air Force with up-to-the-minute weather information.

Code-named 'Pampa' these sorties were a vital element of the assault on Germany. By August 1944 the personnel of 1409 Flight had chalked up an incredible 1,000 Pampa sorties. The unit gave up its Mosquitos when

it moved to Upwood in July 1945 and employed Consolidated Liberators on data-gathering flights deep into the Atlantic until the spring of 1946.

## COOKIES

The Avro Lancaster was not the only aircraft to be able to carry the 4,000lb 'Cookie', or 'block-buster' bomb. Although the cylindrical weapon weighed twice as much as the 'Wooden Wonder's' original bomb capacity, the design team realised, with reduced range, it was possible. The bomb doors were replaced by distinctive bulged versions and these were retrospectively fitted to Mk.IVs and as standard to Mk.IXs and later bomber versions.

On New Year's Day 1944 a new unit came into being at Graveley, Huntingdon. This was 692 Squadron, tasked with perfecting the use of Cookies within the Mosquito force;

**Below**
*Personnel of 1409 Flight in front of a Mosquito IV at Oakington, May 1943.*

**Bottom left**
*The RAF Museum has two Mosquitos, both built as B.25s and converted post-war to TT.35 target-tugs. Displayed at Cosford in the colours of 627 Squadron is TA639, built at Hatfield and put into storage at Shawbury in April 1945. It was converted to a TT.35 in 1952 and served until the final Mosquito tugs were retired at Exeter in May 1963. It was transferred to the care of the museum on July 5, 1967.* RAF MUSEUM
www.rafmuseum.org

its first raid with 4,000-pounders was staged on February 23/24, striking at Dusseldorf. The unit moved to Gransden Lodge in June and disbanded there in September 1945.

As the Lockheed Martin F-35 enters frontline service with the RAF this year, the type's versatility will be emphasised and lauded. It is as well to remember that in 1941 the RAF possessed an aircraft with almost all of the attributes of its 21st century stablemate, including the ultimate 'stealth' material - wood!

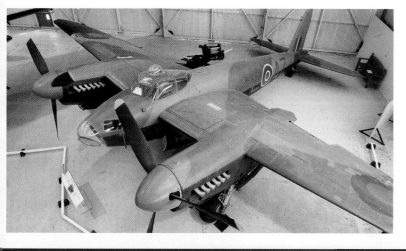

# DOUGLAS
# BOSTON
## 1941 TO 1946

**Above**

*Boston IV BZ511 of 18 Squadron based at Falconara, Italy, mid-1944. Returning to base at night on November 24, 1944 this aircraft stalled on approach and crashed.*

PETE WEST

Ed Heinemann, chief engineer for Douglas, designed a string of successful combat aircraft, from the Dauntless dive-bomber of 1938 through to the A-4 Skyhawk delta wing fighter of 1954. Working at the El Segundo, California, plant, he developed a twin-engined light bomber, the Model 7, in 1938. It was hoped to secure a contract from the United States Army Air Corps.

In February 1939 the French ordered 100 machines based on the Type 7 but demanded many modifications that altered the airframe considerably. The result was the DB-7, and the first example took to the air in August 1939, powered by two 1,200hp (895kW) Pratt & Whitney Twin Wasp radials. The more powerful DB-7A, with a pair of Wright R-2600 Double Cyclones of 1,600hp followed.

With the fall of France in June 1940, undelivered DB-7s and -7As were taken over by the RAF, as Boston Is and IIs, respectively. These were not suitable as light bombers, but Fighter Command was desperate to supplement its night-fighter force. Accordingly, the Havoc programme came about and is detailed in the companion volume, *RAF Centenary Celebration Fighters*.

Additionally, the DB-7B was ordered direct and to British specifications. The first of these was the Boston III, the most numerous variant, with a manually operated gun in the dorsal position. These were followed by the Mk.IV and Mk.V with a power-operated turret, and equivalent of the USAAF A-20G and A-20H Havoc, respectively.

Bostons saw extensive service, based in Britain and following the invasion forces into France, in North

## DOUGLAS BOSTON III

| | |
|---|---|
| **Type:** | Three-crew light bomber |
| **First flight:** | 1938, entered service July 1941 |
| **Powerplant:** | Two 1,600hp (1,193kW) Wright Douglas Cyclone GR-2600 radials |
| **Dimensions:** | Span 61ft 4in (18.69m), Length 47ft 0in (14.32m) |
| **Weights:** | Empty 12,200lb (5,533kg), All-up 25,000lb (11,340kg) |
| **Max speed:** | 304mph (489km/h) at 13,000ft (3,962m) |
| **Range:** | 1,020 miles (1,641km) |
| **Armament:** | Four fixed machine guns in the nose, two each in dorsal and ventral positions. Up to 2,000lb (907kg) of bombs |
| **Replaced:** | Bristol Blenheim from 1941, Martin Baltimore from 1944 |
| **Taken on charge:** | 799, Mk IIIs, IVs and Vs |
| **Replaced by:** | North American Mitchell from 1943, de Havilland Mosquito from 1946 |

Africa, Sicily and Italy. At Swanton Morley, 88 Squadron introduced the Boston to RAF service, beginning replacement of its British Blenheim IVs in July 1941. Moving out of Italy in September 1945, 55 Squadron moved its mix of Boston IVs and Vs to Hassani in Greece. There the unit gave up the RAF's last frontline Bostons in July 1846, re-equipping with de Havilland Mosquito FB.26s.

## INVASION FORCE

On the eve of D-Day, June 5, 1944, the Boston IIIs of 88 and 342 'Lorraine' Squadrons were being prepared for a crucial and dangerous element of the Normandy invasion in which precise positioning and timing were essential. Based at Hartfordbridge – the present-day Blackbushe aerodrome – each aircraft was being fitted with a pair of smoke generators under the belly.

For the men of 342 Squadron the events of the following day had

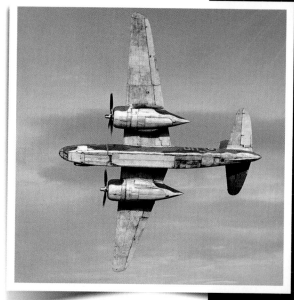

## "Taking off at 05:00, the bombers headed for Normandy... In a carefully choreographed operation, a Boston was to fly low, laying a smoke screen as the landing craft came up the beaches."

huge significance as the unit had been formed in April 1943 from the remnants of French Air Force units evacuated from North Africa. The liberation of their homeland was beginning.

Taking off at 05:00, the bombers headed for Normandy: 88 Squadron was to take the eastern sector, 342 the western side. In a carefully choreographed operation, a Boston was to fly low, laying a smoke screen as the landing craft came up the beaches. Flying a 'racetrack' pattern, another Boston would replace its colleague at ten-minute intervals. Flying low and trailing smoke, the bombers represented a very exposed target for the defending Germans.

Both 88 and 342 both lost

an aircraft, BZ243 and BZ213 respectively crashing into the water close to shoreline, with the three crew on each being killed. Flt Lt O B Smith of 88 Squadron brought his flak-damaged BZ214 *T-for-Tare* back to Hartfordbridge, but it was written off when it crash-landed. Smith and his gunner, Sgt Loake, survived but the navigator, F/Sgt Allan, was killed. Throughout the early hours of the amphibious invasion, 88 and 342 managed to maintain a smoke screen over much of the beachhead.

The two units soon returned to their usual fare, low-level strikes at pinpoint targets. For example, on June 22, two dozen Bostons from 88 and 342 were

engaged in a very successful assault on fortifications near Caen, allowing ground forces to break the impasse and move on.

On October 17, both units touched down at Vitry-en-Artois, east of Arras, from where operations could continue without long 'dead legs' back to Hampshire. At Vitry, 88 Squadron disbanded in April 1945. The Frenchmen did not stay in home territory for long, during that month, 342 began conversion to North American Mitchells ready to re-locate to Gilze-Rijen in Holland before disbanding there in December 1945. ◉

Above, left and right
*Based at Great Massingham, 107 Squadron began to re-equip with Boston IIIs in January 1942, and the opportunity was taken to use AL754 'D-for-Don' for a photo session. On an operation to Eindhoven, Holland, on December 6, 1942, AL754 was badly damaged by flak. The pilot brought the Boston home to Great Massingham, but it overshot on landing and was wrecked.*

Left
*Personnel and Boston IIIs of 88 Squadron parading for the press at Swanton Morley in July 1941.*

# VULTEE
# VENGEANCE

## 1942 TO 1947

**Above**
*Personnel of 'A' Flight
110 Squadron, possibly
at Digri, India in mid-
1943, bedecking a
Vengeance with its dive
brakes deployed.*

**Below**
*A 110 Squadron
Vengeance on a sortie
from Karachi, India,
December 1942.*

Almost any of the fighters featured in our sister publication could become a dive-bomber. The Vultee Vengeance holds a special place in the RAF's heritage as it is the only *dedicated* dive-bomber to have been used operationally.

Conceived to meet a British requirement for a pinpoint, close support aircraft, the Vultee took into account early war experience, especially the potential exhibited by the Junkers Ju 87 'Stuka'. The Vengeance carried an impressive warload of up to 2,000lb (907kg) – in the early 1930s, which would have categorised it as a *heavy* bomber.

Orders for a British version of the V-72 were placed in mid-1940 and the first example had its maiden flight at Nashville, Tennessee, in July 1941. Many modifications were needed, and it was not until June 1942 that the initial production example was ready for delivery. Vultee was faced with problems gearing up for mass manufacture and Northrop at Hawthorne, California, also built Vengeances for the RAF.

Frontline Vengeances were almost exclusively issued to the India-Burma theatre where, after teething troubles, the type excelled in the close support role. Four RAF squadrons, 45, 82, 84 and 110 flew Vengeances, with the air forces of Australia and India also using the type in the region.

The first operational RAF Vengeance unit was 82 Squadron, initially at Karachi (in present-day Pakistan), in August 1942. It was the following spring before the dive-bombers were ready for combat. The Vengeance's time in action was relatively brief, 84 Squadron was the last to fly the type operationally, in July 1944.

Vultee's dive-bomber found another role with the RAF, the vital and often dangerous work of target towing. Contractor Cunliffe-Owen Aircraft devised the conversion and nine British-based units flew the tug, the first of which was 587 Squadron at Weston Zoyland. The target-tug version was the last to fly for the RAF; the final examples were retired in May 1947.

### TERMINAL VELOCITY
In his superb feature *Devastation to Order,* in the September 2016 edition of *FlyPast,* Sean Feast paid tribute to the unsung Vengeance. Wg Cdr Dennis Gibbs was the commanding officer of 82 Squadron, the first unit to receive the dive-bomber. Gibbs and his men had to battle with serviceability problems and it was not until April 1943 before the unit was fully operational.

"Early Vengeance sorties comprised sea patrols, hunting with little success for elusive Japanese submarines. The squadron also experimented with tactics, including the optimum formations, the ideal length of dive and angle of attack.

"'Vics' of up to a dozen aircraft were considered ideal, diving from 10,000ft (3,048m) to achieve an accurate drop and allowing a suitable margin to descend lower if required. Terminal velocity, with dive brakes extended and one-third throttle, was recorded as 320mph (514km/h) at 90°, or 290mph at 75°. Pilots were soon getting the hang of things, some being able to place their bombs within 15 yards (13.7m) of the objective.

"The crews of 110 Squadron celebrated a red-letter day on March 19, 1943 when a box of six Vengeances bombed a Japanese headquarters in Htizwe village on the Arakan Front in Burma.

> "Terminal velocity, with dive brakes extended and one-third throttle, was recorded as 320mph at 90°... Pilots were soon getting the hang of things, some being able to place their bombs within 15 yards of the objective."

Supporting Allied troops who were heavily engaged, all 12 bombs burst in the centre of the target, causing considerable damage.

"An unusual task was a precision strike on a photo-recce Spitfire that had crashed behind enemy lines. The Allies did not want its camera equipment falling into Japanese hands so 45 Squadron was ordered to destroy it."

On October 17, 1943, Flt Sgt

**Left**
A profile view of the wing layout of the Vengeance, albeit on a damaged print.

Richard Harding (23) and his navigator, W/O John Barnard, of 82 Squadron failed to return. They were the first combat casualties of any RAF Vengeance unit.

## CAB RANK

"As well as frontline objectives, Vengeance units were also briefed to support the behind-the-lines activities of the famed General Orde Wingate and his 'Chindit' special forces. When the first columns moved off, 84 Squadron, under Sqn Ldr Arthur Gill, was ready to give cover and was soon relieved by his counterparts in 45 Squadron.

"Increasingly, the RAF units worked alongside one another in a pattern not dissimilar to the 'cab rank' system perfected by Hawker Typhoon squadrons over Northern Europe.

"Flak remained the greatest danger. Japanese fighters appeared only occasionally, but when danger was expected the dive-bombers flew with fighter escort – but that was no means a given. Vengeances mostly had to fend for themselves.

"With increased liaison with ground forces, Vengeances could drop down from the skies to pick off targets where they were most needed. For example, on January 17, 1944 two dozen Vengeances from 45 and 110 Squadrons attacked a Japanese stronghold at Kyauktaw twice in the space of less than 20 minutes, with devastating effect." ◎

**Above**
An impressive bomb tally on an 82 Squadron Vengeance.

**Left**
Bombing up an 82 Squadron Vengeance at Jumchar, India, in the spring of 1944.
ALL KEC

## VULTEE VENGEANCE I

| | |
|---|---|
| Type: | Two-seat dive-bomber |
| First flight: | March 1941, entered service August 1942 |
| Powerplant: | One 1,700hp (1,268kW) Wright Double Cyclone GR-2600 radial |
| Dimensions: | Span 48ft 0in (14.63m), Length 40ft 0in (12.19m) |
| Weights: | Empty 10,300lb (4,672kg), All-up 16,400lb (7,439kg) |
| Max speed: | 279mph (448km/h) at 14,000ft (4,267m) |
| Range: | 1,200 miles (1,931km) |
| Armament: | Two machine guns in each wing, two in rear position. Up to 2,000lb (907kg) of bombs |
| Replaced: | In dive-bomber role only: Bristol Blenheim IV from 1942 |
| Taken on charge: | 1,205 including 400 built by Northrop |
| Replaced by: | De Havilland Mosquito from 1944 |

# LOCKHEED
# VENTURA
## 1941 TO 1944

Originating as a mailplane for Imperial Airways, the Avro Anson became a reliable coastal reconnaissance aircraft and went on to an exceptional production and service career as a trainer and transport. The same idea was applied to the Lockheed Super Electra twin which morphed into the Hudson maritime patroller in 1938.

Learning from the Hudson the larger, more powerful Lodestar was militarised as the Ventura and this had its maiden flight on July 31, 1941. This new aircraft was intended to be much more aggressive than the Hudson, and Bomber Command saw it as a potent attack aircraft. It was well into the spring of 1942 before Lockheed had perfected the Ventura and geared up for mass production. That time lag was to be detrimental to the type's effectiveness as a bomber.

Withdrawn from Bomber Command's frontline in September 1943, Venturas found a niche as light bombers in North Africa and the Middle East. The GR.V maritime reconnaissance version, the equivalent of the US Navy's much improved PV-1, enjoyed some success with Coastal Command. By 1944 the Ventura was phased out, yet its forebear, the Hudson, continued in service until August 1945.

## HUNG UP
Feltwell-based 464 Squadron Royal Australian Air Force contributed to a force of 60 Venturas sent to Dunkirk on February 26, 1943. Among them was Mk.II AJ224 *N-for-Nun* of 'B' Flight, piloted by Sqn Ldr I Dale. The target was a warship in the harbour; 33 of the Venturas bombed, all returned to their bases.

Having declared 'bombs gone' a burst of flak hit the nose of AJ224 and shards of Perspex hit Dale and Fg Off H Robson DFM, both of whom were temporarily blinded.

Dale recovered, and they set course for base where *Nun* belly landed at 15:30. Dale and Robson, drenched in blood were hospitalised. The other two crew, Canadian Fg Off G Forman and Australian Plt Off J

Quinlan were unhurt.

The Ventura was declared a write-off and during salvage it became clear how lucky the crew had been. Two 500-pounders had hung up in the bomb bay, but thankfully behaved themselves.

*Right Down on its belly at Feltwell, Ventura II AJ224 of 464 Squadron RAAF after a harrowing flight back from raiding Dunkirk, February 26, 1943.* KEC

*Below right A famous image of Lockheed Hudson III T9465 of Iceland-based 269 Squadron in 1941. It carries the legend 'Spirit of Lockheed-Vega Employees' along the fuselage – it was paid for by donations from the factory at Burbank, California.* LOCKHEED

## CARNAGE AT LOW-LEVEL
Just before noon on December 6, 1942 a force of 93 bombers took off on Operation 'Oyster', bound for the Philips electronics factory in the middle of the Dutch town of Eindhoven. The armada comprised nine de Havilland Mosquito bombers, a Mosquito for photo-recce, 36 Douglas Bostons and 47 Venturas – 17 from 21 Squadron at Methwold, 14 from 464 Squadron Royal Australian Air Force and 16 from 487 Squadron Royal New Zealand Air Force, both based at Feltwell.

It was Sunday and dinner time and the plan was to minimise casualties in the civilian workforce. The bombers went in at low level and the flak was intense. As the stragglers peeled away it was clear the target had taken a pasting; it was six months before production returned to normal. Despite the hopes that losses could be kept small, 148 Dutch factory workers and seven German military personnel died in the attack.

One Mosquito and four Bostons failed to return. At Feltwell and Methwold, streams of Venturas returned, many with flak damage. One had its wing leading edge badly

mauled when it flew through a tree. Three Venturas force-landed upon return.

As well as Luftwaffe fighters and German anti-aircraft fire, Mother Nature played a part in the carnage – 23 Venturas had suffered bird strikes, some multiple with crippling consequences.

Nine Venturas never made it back – an horrific 19% of the force dispatched. Each of the squadrons

lost three aircraft; five aircrew of 21 Squadron died and another three became prisoners of war; 12 were killed in 487 and eight died and four became prisoners of war with 464.

Sgt A V Ricketts and his crew of three from 21 Squadron nursed AE687 *P-for-Pip* back across the North Sea, but just 7 miles (11.2km) off the Suffolk coast had to ditch. An air-sea rescue launch out of Felixstowe picked the quartet up.

## LOCKHEED VENTURA II

| | |
|---|---|
| **Type:** | Five-crew light bomber |
| **First flight:** | July 31, 1941, Mk.I entered service May 1942 |
| **Powerplant:** | Two 2,000hp (1,492kW) Pratt & Whitney Double Wasp GR-2800 radials |
| **Dimensions:** | Span 65ft 6in (19.96m), Length 51ft 2in (15.59m) |
| **Weights:** | Empty 17,250lb (7,824kg), All-up 26,000lb (11,793kg) |
| **Max speed:** | 302mph (486km/h) at 18,000ft (5,486m) |
| **Range:** | 950 miles (1,528km) |
| **Armament:** | Two fixed machine guns in the nose plus two movable from forward to 30° downwards, two in dorsal turret, two in ventral position. Up to 2,500lb (1,134kg) of bombs |
| **Replaced:** | Bristol Blenheim from 1942, Lockheed Hudson from 1943 |
| **Taken on charge:** | 678 plus transfers to South African Air Force |
| **Replaced by:** | De Havilland Mosquito from 1943, Martin Baltimore from 1944 |

## "As well as Luftwaffe fighters and German anti-aircraft fire, Mother Nature played a part in the carnage – 23 Venturas had suffered bird strikes..."

Worse was to come. On May 3, 1943, while attacking a power station near Amsterdam, 11 Venturas were lost.

The Lockheed's limitations as a bomber were all too obvious and the type was withdrawn from Bomber Command's order of battle in September.

By the time the Ventura had entered service it was outclassed. Crews found that while they were pleasant to fly they lacked agility, especially at low level.

It was not often that RAF pilots bestowed derogatory nicknames on their aircraft, but to many the Lockheed twin was 'The Pig'. ◉

**Above left**
*Delivered to Britain in 1943, Ventura I FN957/G was issued directly to the Telecommunications Flying Unit at Defford. This probably explains the '/G' suffix to its serial number, which denoted it should be placed under guard whenever left idle. It is illustrated while under evaluation at the Aeroplane and Armament Experimental Establishment at Boscombe Down, fitted with a Martin CE250 low-profile turret and drop tanks.*

**Below**
*Ventura Is of 21 Squadron being introduced to the press at Bodney, May 1942.*
PETER GREEN COLLECTION

# MARTIN MARAUDER

## 1942 TO 1946

**Right**
*Large numbers of Marauders ordered by the RAF retained their USAAF serial on the fin and rudder: Mk.II FB431 wears 135362 showing it was a B-26C built at Martin's Omaha, Nebraska, factory. Serving with 12 Squadron South African Air Force FB431 was at Foggia, Italy, in early 1944.* KEC

**Right centre**
*Approved by King George VI in May 1937, the badge of 14 Squadron represents a crusader in association with the Cross of St George. The Arabic motto translates as 'I spread my wings and keep my promise'.*

'Baltimore Whore' or 'Flying Prostitute' were nicknames bestowed upon the early Martin B-26 Marauders by American aircrew. With its very high wing loading producing fast approach speeds, vicious responses near the stall and a string of fatal propeller failures, the bomber from Baltimore, Maryland, was also known as the 'Martin Murderer', 'Crew Killer' or the 'Widow Maker'.

The names relating to 'ladies of the night' were concerned with aerodynamics, not morality. With its all-up weight of 30,000lb, a B-26A was close to that of a Wellington I, but the Martin had a wing area of 602sq ft (55.92m$^2$) and a span of 65ft 0in (19.8m) whereas the Vickers product measured up at 840sq ft and 86ft 2in, respectively. With that relatively small wing doing all the work, the Marauder looked as though it had "no visible means of support"!

The first Marauders for the RAF were the equivalent of the short-span B-26A, but the Mk.IIs and IIIs featured the extended 71ft span. This, along with engine and propeller improvements, turned the aircraft into a very capable medium bomber. Many Marauders were handed on to the South African Air Force and these worked alongside their RAF colleagues in North Africa, into Sicily and through the Italian campaign.

Only two RAF frontline units flew the Marauder. Replacing Bristol Blenheim Vs, 14 Squadron took its first examples in August 1942, but it was not until October 28 that the unit became operational. As well as medium-level bombing, the unit carried out torpedo attacks, mine laying, anti-submarine patrols and shipping reconnaissance sorties across North Africa and to targets as far as Italy and Greece. The last Marauder operation undertaken by 14 was on September 21, 1944 after which Wellington XIVs were introduced.

In December 1944 at Biferno in Italy, 39 Squadron converted to Marauders, having previously flown Bristol Beauforts. The unit's main task was to support partisans in Yugoslavia, across the Adriatic Sea, but anti-shipping strikes were also staged. The last 'op' was flown on May 4, 1945 and 39 Squadron redeployed to Khartoum, Sudan, where its Marauders were retired in September 1946 and de Havilland Mosquito FB.26s were adopted.

For a brief while, both 14 and 39 Squadrons flew anti-shipping strikes with the 2,000lb (907kg) torpedoes – the B-26 was designed for this task from the outset. Neither unit had great success in this role.

### MARTIN MARAUDER III

| | |
|---|---|
| **Type:** | Six-crew medium bomber |
| **First flight:** | November 25, 1940, entered service August 1942 |
| **Powerplant:** | Two 2,000hp (1,492kW) Pratt & Whitney Double Wasp R-2800 radials |
| **Dimensions:** | Span 71ft 0in (21.64m), Length 57ft 6in (17.52m) |
| **Weights:** | Empty 24,000lb (10,886kg), All-up 37,000lb (16,783kg) |
| **Max speed:** | 305mph (490km/h) at 15,000ft (4,572m) |
| **Range:** | 1,200 miles (1,931km) |
| **Armament:** | One fixed and one free-mounted machine gun in the nose, two machine guns in dorsal turret and tail position. One machine gun in port and starboard beam positions. Up to 4,000lb (1,814kg) of bombs |
| **Replaced:** | Bristol Blenheim in 1942 (14 Squadron); Bristol Beaufort in 1944 (39 Squadron) |
| **Taken on charge:** | About 366, plus transfers to the South African Air Force |
| **Replaced by:** | Vickers Wellington in 1944 (14 Squadron); de Havilland Mosquito in 1946 (39 Squadron) |

## CRUSADERS

Gil Graham was a tail gunner on 14 Squadron's Marauders and through the unit's association journal *The Old Crusader*, he wrote of his experiences. He flew with Wg Cdr Dick Maydwell, the rest of the crew comprising: Bill Pratt (second pilot), F Kennedy (navigator), Bob Sutton (wireless operator) and Titch Lacker (mid-upper gunner).

"The policy was that vital military targets in Rome should be bombed by a combined force of RAF and US bombers. The problem was that the Vatican and other most holy places in the city were *not* to be touched.

"In order to be absolutely certain of this, it was decided that a Marauder of 14 Squadron would fly to the target area on the morning of the raid, check the weather conditions and radio the results back to base. Only if the weather was perfect would the raid take place.

"So, on the 19th July, 1943

Marauder I FK142 *R-for-Robert*, named *Dominion Triumph,* with Dick Maydwell at the controls, took off from our base at Protville in Tunisia at 03:00 hours, well before dawn. Flying at our operational height of 50ft [we] headed across the Mediterranean for Rome hoping that we would not be picked up by enemy radar.

"A few minutes after crossing the Italian coast near Anzio when we found ourselves streaking across an enemy field at deck level doing around 260mph. So surprised were we that I didn't have time to open up on a row of Heinkel He 111 bombers all neatly lined up alongside the runway.

"We got to the target area where the weather was indeed perfect and even though this was around dawn, we were certain that cloud would not develop later in the day. The information was immediately radioed back to base.

"We flew over the target area and continued to fly north, and to our

delight came to Lake Bracciano where we noticed a number of seaplanes anchored. By now we had completed the essential part of our mission [so] Dick decided we would try to knock out one or two of the seaplanes. We flew down right alongside and I opened up on them and saw some strikes hit. Reconnaissance the next day showed at least three badly damaged and lying on their side in the water.

"A few minutes later we came across a goods train, so we strafed it as well, but couldn't assess our results. We now turned due west and headed for open sea, but as we crossed the coast I noticed considerable numbers of fighters at a higher altitude – fortunately we ran into a bank of sea fog before they saw us. This provided us with excellent cover until we were off the coast of Sardinia when we turned south and headed for home, where we arrived at 08:10 just in time for breakfast." ◉

**Top**
*Rare in-flight image of Marauders of 39 Squadron.*

**Above**
*Marauder IA FK375 'Dominion Revenge' of 14 Squadron, as flown by Wg Cdr Dick Maydwell. This machine failed to return from a strike on a convoy off the Aghios Giorgios Islands, in the Aegean Sea south of Athens, on July 20, 1943.* PETE WEST

**Below**
*A torpedo-equipped Marauder of 14 Squadron in 1943 at North Africa. It is one of the machines flown by Wg Cdr Dick Maydwell.* KEC

# NORTH AMERICAN
# MITCHELL
## 1942 TO 1949

**Above**
*A line-up of Mk.IIs of 180 Squadron Dunsfold during the summer of 1943. The aircraft second from the camera, FL707, carries '133' on the nose.*

While poring over countless air-to-ground images at Medmenham in Buckinghamshire on November 13, 1943, RAF photo-interpreter Constance Babington Smith spotted a little aircraft on the airfield at Karlshagen, near Peenemünde on Germany's Baltic coast. She had discovered the V-1 'Doodle-bug' and eventually linked it with the mysterious 'ski ramps' to be found nearby.

The little unguided flying-bomb was the first of Hitler's 'revenge' weapons and the RAF 2nd Tactical Air Force was tasked with disrupting its deployment. The launch ramps and associated infrastructure were impossible to hide, but difficult to put out of action and bristled with anti-aircraft guns.

In November 1943 Operation 'Crossbow' was designated as the campaign against all forms of German long-range weaponry. (This name inspired the title of the 1965 Michael Anderson film *Operation Crossbow*, starring George Peppard, about a clandestine raid on a V-2 missile plant.)

On November 26, RAF Mitchells were sent to Martinvast, south of Cherbourg, France, to hit a suspected V-1 launch site. Three units, Dunsfold-based 98 and 180 Squadrons and the Dutch 320 Squadron, operating from Lasham, met withering flak over the target.

Three aircraft of 180 Squadron were shot down, each with a crew of four, all of whom died. Sgt J A Kok, piloting FR146, *O-for-Oboe*, of 320 Squadron did his best to control the bomber after it was hit by accurate flak and attempted a crash-landing near the target. He and another died in the wreck. Sgts Koning and Overwijn scrambled away; the former was taken prisoner, but Overwijn succeeded in a 'home run', evading through Spain.

In December the code-word 'Noball' came into use to denote sorties that were striking at V-weapon sites. By the end of the month massed raids were organised, for example on December 22 a force of 35 bombers, comprising Douglas Bostons, de Havilland Mosquitos and Mitchells were sent to three Noball objectives.

A dozen Mitchells, from 98 and 180 Squadrons, were tasked with attacking a construction at St Pierre de Jonquières, east of Dieppe. Post-strike reconnaissance images seldom revealed if a site had been destroyed, but once it became clear the Doodle-bugs were to be launched off ramps, the tactics applied to Noball targets could be perfected. (It was June 13, 1944 before the first wave of V-1s was sent towards London.)

W/O D Rogers eased Mitchell II FL218 *W-for-William* of 180 Squadron – featured as artwork and in flight on these pages – off the runway at Dunsfold, just after 09:00 hours on January 24, 1944. There were seven bomb tallies proudly painted near the cockpit, as was

a red griffin and the Latin legend 'Nulli Secundus' – second to none.

The objective for the Dunsfold-based 98 and 180 Squadrons was a Noball site near Cherbourg. The Mitchell was seriously damaged by flak, but Rogers coaxed the aircraft back across the Channel. Having made landfall on the Kent coast, three of the crew successfully baled out. Rogers attempted to crash-land FL218, bringing it down not far from the airfield at Hawkinge; he was killed.

## TACTICAL ROLE

Beyond doubt the finest American medium bomber of World War Two, 9,816 North American B-25 Mitchells were built up to 1945. A large number of air arms used B-25s post-war; the USAF continued to use the type as a crew trainer and staff transport.

As the Mitchell developed, the RAF ordered newer versions, the initial Mk.Is and IIs being based on the B-25C and 'D, while the Mk.III was based on the B-25J. At West Raynham 98 Squadron was the first to accept the Mitchell for operations, followed closely by 180 Squadron, in September 1942. Both units relocated to Dunsfold in August 1943.

Mitchells were used almost exclusively in the tactical role, as related in the example above. Initially based in Britain, they moved into continental Europe after D-Day. As well as 98 and 180, they

## NORTH AMERICAN MITCHELL II

| | |
|---|---|
| **Type:** | Five-crew medium bomber |
| **First flight:** | January 1939, entered service September 1942 |
| **Powerplant:** | Two 1,700hp (1,268kW) Wright Double Cyclone GR-2600 radial |
| **Dimensions:** | Span 67ft 7in (20.63m), Length 54ft 1in (16.48m) |
| **Weights:** | Empty 16,000lb (7,257kg), All-up 26,000lb (11.793kg) |
| **Max speed:** | 292mph (469km/h) at 15,000ft (4,572m) |
| **Range:** | 1,230 miles (1,979km) |
| **Armament:** | One free-mounted machine gun in the nose, two in dorsal turret and ventral position. Up to 4,000lb (1,814kg) of bombs |
| **Replaced:** | Douglas Boston, Lockheed Hudson and Vickers Wellington from 1943 |
| **Taken on charge:** | 844 |
| **Replaced by:** | De Havilland Mosquitos from 1945 |

were flown by 226, 305 (Polish) 320 (Dutch) and 342 (French) Squadrons. The Mitchell was retired as a bomber with the RAF in May 1945.

### EMPIRE MITCHELL

Almost certainly the last Mitchell in service with the RAF was still flying in 1949 as part of the Empire Flying School's eclectic fleet based at Hullavington. Built in 1944 and initially serving with the Aeroplane and Armament Experimental Establishment at Boscombe Down, Mk.II FR209 was issued to the Empire Central Flying School (ECFS) in early 1945.

With so many nationalities working

within the RAF, ECFS was established in 1942 to co-ordinate and improve training standards across the many schools in the UK, Canada, Africa and the USA.

In May 1946 ECFS was renamed as the Empire Flying School and continued to function at Hullavington until July 31, 1949 when it was disbanded. By 1947 Mitchell FR209 had forsaken camouflage and was flying in an overall natural metal finish. This venerable survivor was finally struck off charge in September 1951.

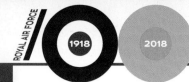

# AVRO
# LINCOLN

## 1945 TO 1963

**Above**
*A Lincoln II without squadron markings in 1946 wearing the white and black 'Tiger Force' colours in which the type would have gone to war against Japan.*

By the time of D-Day, June 6, 1944, strategic planning was already in hand about how the war against Japan would be concluded. Bomber Command was to contribute what became known as 'Tiger Force', initially equipped with Lancasters modified for use in the Far East. A more powerful and bigger Lancaster was required and designer Roy Chadwick turned his team to making a 'super' version.

This programme was at first designated Lancaster IV and V with Rolls-Royce or Packard-built Merlins, respectively. As much of the Lancaster was included in the new type as possible in order to speed development, the resulting bomber's heritage was obvious.

Span was extended from the Lancaster I's 102ft 0in (31m) to 120ft 0in and length grew from 69ft 4in to 78ft 3in. The Lancaster's Merlin 22s were rated at 1,280hp (954kW) while the new type had Merlin 85s of 1,750hp. All-up weight increased dramatically, from 49,950lb (22,657kg) to 82,000lb.

Just as the Manchester III needed a new name – Lancaster – to emphasise how different it was from its predecessor, so the Lancaster IV and V had to adopt a new label. Keeping to the county town theme, it was called Lincoln, reflecting the region from which so many Lancasters were despatched.

Test pilot 'Sam' Brown was at the helm for the maiden flight of the prototype, PW925, from Ringway on June 9, 1944. In the same month that Japan surrendered, August 1945, the first Lincolns were issued to 57 Squadron at East Kirkby. Lincolns went on to be Bomber Command's post-war mainstay until the early

| AVRO LINCOLN I | |
|---|---|
| **Type:** | Seven crew heavy bomber |
| **First flight:** | June 9, 1944, entered service August 1945 |
| **Powerplant:** | Four 1,680hp (1,253kW) Rolls-Royce Merlin 85 V12s |
| **Dimensions:** | Span 120ft 0in (36.57m), Length 78ft 3¼in (23.85m) |
| **Weights:** | Empty 43,400lb (19,686kg), All-up 82,000lb (37,195kg) |
| **Max speed:** | 295mph (474km/h) at 15,000ft (4,572m) |
| **Range:** | 1,470 miles (2,365km) |
| **Armament:** | Two machine guns in nose, mid-upper and tail turrets. Up to 14,000lb (6,350kg) of bombs |
| **Replaced:** | Avro Lancaster from 1946 |
| **Taken on charge:** | 529 |
| **Replaced by:** | Boeing Washington from 1950, English Electric Canberra from 1951 |

1950s when the jet-powered English Electric Canberra took over.

In total, 529 Lincolns were ordered for the RAF and a small number served with the Argentine Air Force. A single example was built in Canada and the Government Aircraft Factory at Fishermens Bend, Melbourne, made 54 Mk.30s for the Royal Australian Air Force (RAAF).

## SLEDGEHAMMERS

While the Lincoln did not see action in World War Two, it was used to combat guerrilla forces in Kenya and Malaya. Based at Eastleigh, Nairobi, detachments of Lincolns attacked the Mau Mau 1953 to 1954 – see page 3. The big bombers had a limited effect in this conflict, being described as "like using a sledgehammer to crack a walnut" by an armourer from 100 Squadron.

Famously understated as the 'Emergency', the struggle with communist insurgents in Malaya was waged, ultimately to success, from 1948 to 1960. Detachments of Lincolns were introduced to the

region in March 1950, based at Tengah, Singapore. The first raid was staged on the 26th.

Terrorist camps and supply dumps located deep in the dense and vast Malayan jungle were more appropriate targets for the 'sledgehammers'. The unsophisticated 1,000lb bomb was used to devastating effect, each Lincoln carrying 14 in its huge weapons bay. Detonations within a wooded area generated shockwaves and countless wooden shards caused considerable damage to the makeshift guerrilla installations.

When conditions permitted, up to five Lincolns flying in close formation at relatively low level could inflict massive damage to manpower, materiel and morale. These tactics forced the enemy to abandon large bases and disperse its forces into smaller groups, greatly reducing its combat ability.

From June 1950 RAAF Lincolns arrived at Tengah to take part in operations. The RAF withdrew the type from March 1955 when Canberras took over. The RAAF kept

its Lincolns in theatre until February 1956.

The last RAF examples were employed by 151 Squadron at Watton on radio and radar development trials. The final trio operational with 151 flew a farewell formation on March 12, 1963. One of the participants was RF398, now on display at the RAF Museum at Cosford.

## 40 YEARS OF SERVICE

A Mk.III Lincoln for air-sea rescue and maritime patrol was initiated by Chadwick and his team, but this was sidelined in favour of a more comprehensive solution. A shorter, but more capacious, fuselage was mated to a Lincoln wing, with four 2,450hp Rolls-Royce Griffon 57As driving counter-rotating propellers. This emerged as the Shackleton, not strictly a bomber in the sense of this publication, but such an important type in RAF heritage and in the story of the Manchester-Lancaster-Lincoln that it *must* get a mention.

Jimmy Orrell carried out the inaugural flight of the prototype, VW126, on March 9, 1949 and the RAF received its first Shackleton GR.1 (later MR.1) in April 1951. Production totalled 178 in three major variants; the last coming off the line in 1959.

As a stopgap, an airborne early warning version, the Shackleton AEW.2 was created. The first conversion, WL745, flew at Woodford on September 30, 1971 and was followed by 11 more. The fleet soldiered on until July 1, 1991 – Shackleton had clocked a staggering 40 years of service. ◎

# BRISTOL
# BRIGAND

## 1949 TO 1958

From the Blenheim to the Beaufort and on to the superlative Beaufighter, Bristol had created an enviable line of warplanes. All this expertise needed to be capitalised upon and the Filton design house began work on a new type in early 1941, coming up with the Buckingham, a four-crew bomber with a 4,000lb (1,814kg) weapon load.

The prototype had its maiden flight on February 4, 1943 but by then it had missed the boat. The amazing de Havilland Mosquito out-performed the Buckingham and the North American Mitchell was showing considerable promise.

The Buckingham had already entered limited production and a small number found a niche as high-speed transports. An advanced trainer version, the Buckmaster, was also built, some of these serving until 1958.

Even something as good as the Beaufighter would need replacement eventually and in 1943 Bristol began to address this need. The Beaufighter has essentially been a slimline, fighter-like fuselage, married to the wings and tail of its Beaufort forebear. The same logic was used to conceive the Brigand and the prototype first flew on December 4, 1944.

Like the Buckingham, time ran out for the Brigand as by the end of the war air-launched torpedo warfare was facing extinction.

After a small run of TF.I torpedo-bombers, none of which entered operational service, Filton switched to building B.I light bomber versions. For the RAF, the Brigand was the last of its kind, a piston-engined attack aircraft.

(During 1948 RAF and Fleet Air Arm designations changed from Roman to Arabic numerals; the Brigand becoming the B.1.)

Brigands entered RAF frontline service at Habbaniya, Iraq, with 84 Squadron in June 1949. Only two more squadrons were to be equipped, 45 and 85, both of which went to war in Malaya.

Brigands were also used for weather reconnaissance and, as T.4s and T.5s, crew trainers. The last examples were retired from 238 Operational Conversion Unit at North Luffenham in March 1958.

## FIREDOG

With its four 20mm cannon and able to carry up to 3,000lb (1,360kg) of munitions, including 80lb rocket projectiles, the Brigand was considered an ideal for use in Operation 'Firedog', the long-running conflict against communist guerrillas in Malaya. The B.1s of 84 Squadron

| BRISTOL BRIGAND B.I | |
|---|---|
| **Type:** | Three-crew light bomber |
| **First flight:** | December 4, 1944, entered service June 1949 |
| **Powerplant:** | One 2,470hp (1,842kW) Bristol Centaurus 57 radials |
| **Dimensions:** | Span 72ft 4in (22.04m), Length 46ft 5in (14.14m) |
| **Weights:** | Empty 25,598lb (11,611kg), All-up 39,000lb (17,690kg) |
| **Max speed:** | 358mph (576km/h) at 16,000ft (4,876m) |
| **Range:** | 2,800 miles (4,506km) |
| **Armament:** | Four 20mm cannon in the nose. Up to 3,000lb (1,360kg) of bombs |
| **Replaced:** | Bristol Beaufighter and Hawker Tempest from 1949 |
| **Taken on charge:** | 142 |
| **Replaced by:** | De Havilland Hornet from 1951 and de Havilland Vampire from 1952 |

broke off and the Brigand plummeted into the jungle, killing all three crew.

Investigations asserted that the mainspar had probably crystallised; yet another of the structural problems that had plagued the type's career. Other alarming incidents included what a Brigand groundcrew member called "the ultimate engine failure" a Centaurus radial falling from its mounts  and propeller blades, or entire assemblies, flying off. With RH823's horrific accident, the Brigand was withdrawn from frontline operations.

Brigand RH823, which was built at Filton, was tested prior to issue to the RAF in the late summer of 1948. On October 14 the very next machine off the production line, RH824, was

settled into Tengah, Singapore, in February 1949 and they were joined by 45 Squadron in December.

With a huge area to police, Brigands and other types were used mostly in flights of three or four, but by mid-1951 large formations, designed to intimidate and scatter terrorist forces, were increasingly adopted.

On September 12, 1951 a trio of Brigands struck at a suspected large encampment at Kuala Selangor, on Malaya's western coast, north of Kuala Lumpur. Intelligence and reconnaissance revealed that the area was indeed a major base and on November 8, a show of force was organised. In a series of strikes 14 Brigands, eight de Havilland Hornets, four Avro Lincolns (see page 76) and a solitary Short Sunderland laid waste to the bandit camp.

Sunderland flying-boats of 205 Squadron, based at Seletar, Singapore, and operating from the Straits of Johor, proved to be very efficient anti-insurgent aircraft, with good firepower from the turrets and a 2,000lb bomb load and, most advantageous, it ability

to loiter awaiting 'trade'.

The Brigand fleet was becoming more and more prone to accidents and 45 Squadron traded them in for another piston twin, the Hornet, in January 1952. This left 84 Squadron sticking with the type, but all this came to a rapid halt on December 20.

Pilot Flt Lt Brendan Massey, navigator Sgt Edward Powell and LAC Douglas Kay were airborne in B.1 RH823 over Kota Tinggi in southern Malaya. As Massey pulled RH823 out of a shallow dive, the starboard wing

taken up by Bristol test pilot Sqn Ldr Douglas Weightman DFC ready for sign off. The port Centaurus failed and the propeller blades sheared off, impacting in the nose section and starboard engine.

Weightman was over a populated area, he struggled with the controls to take the doomed Brigand to the northwest. Attempting to force-land at Northwick, on the shores of the River Severn, he was killed when RH824 hit trees. Brigands had been trouble from beginning to end. ◎

**Above**
*Rocket-equipped Brigand B.1 VS814 of 8 Squadron, based at Khormaksar, Aden, 1949. It was written off in a belly landing at Shaibah, Iraq, on July 4, 1951 when the undercarriage refused to come down.* PETE WEST

**Above left**
*Brigand T.5 RH797 of 238 Operational Conversion Unit, North Luffenham, 1957.* KEC

**Left**
*Early production Buckingham I, KV335, in 1945. Like most of the Mk.Is, it saw no RAF service.* BRISTOL

**Below left**
*Brigand B.1 of 8 Squadron at Khormaksar, Aden, in 1950.* PETER GREEN COLLECTION

# BOEING
# WASHINGTON

## 1950 TO 1958

**Right**
*The flight deck of the Washington was spacious and generously glazed. The two pilots sat well back from the windscreen, with the bomb aimer – complete with a famous Norden bomb sight – in the extreme nose.*
KEC

the Boeing plant at Wichita, Kansas, in 1944; the other three were much the same age, but had emerged from the Renton, Washington state, factory. These machines were to form the basis of the Washington Conversion Unit (WCU) at Marham, to get all aircrew used to the foibles of the B-29.

### VETERAN BOMBER
Crews trained by the WCU were ready to inaugurate the 'new' bomber into frontline service in June 1950 when 115 Squadron accepted its first

I t wasn't a good start. As the first B-29 was spotted on approach, it was obvious the starboard inner engine had been feathered and oil was streaming out of the nacelle. After it had taxied in, close inspection of the airframe revealed patches; the bomber had been hit by anti-aircraft fire and been repaired, but with little finesse. The RAF had been reduced to accepting well-used hand-me-downs.

Announced in January 1950 and achieved with great speed, the USA was lending Boeing B-29 Superfortresses to the RAF under the Mutual Defense Assistance Program. The Berlin blockade had ended in May 1948 and the Cold War had become a harsh reality. Bomber Command's mainstay, the Avro Lincoln, had limitations and Britain's strategic forces needed bolstering.

The Washingtons provided a stopgap before the planned V-bombers entered service. Their appearance was fortuitous, five months later the Korean War broke out and the world braced itself for another global conflict.

Brought out of storage, the first four of what the 'Brits' called the Washington B.1, were ferried to Andrews Air Force Base, Maryland,

## BOEING WASHINGTON B.I

| Type: | Ten-crew heavy bomber |
|---|---|
| First flight: | September 21, 1942, entered service June 1950 |
| Powerplant: | Four 2,200hp (1,641kW) Wright Cyclone R-3350 radials |
| Dimensions: | Span 141ft 3in (43.05m), Length 99ft 0in (30.17m) |
| Weights: | Empty 74,500lb (33,793kg), All-up 120,000lb (54,432kg) |
| Max speed: | 350mph (563km/h) at 25,000ft (7,620m) |
| Range: | 2,850 miles (4,586km) |
| Armament: | Two machine guns in remotely controlled fore and aft upper, and fore and aft lower turrets. Two machine guns in tail position. Up to 17,500lb (7,938kg) of bombs |
| Replaced: | Avro Lincoln from 1950 |
| Taken on charge: | 88 |
| Replaced by: | English Electric Canberra from 1953 |

for a brief handover ceremony on March 20, 1950. Crews from the 307th Bomb Wing brought the quartet of Boeings across the Atlantic and they arrived in the circuit at Marham on the 22nd where more speeches and handshaking awaited.

It was B-29-55-BW 44-69680 – the prospective WF437 – that suffered the glitch and needed to feather the massive four-bladed propeller on its 2,200hp (1,641kW) Wright Cyclone R-3350 radial. It had been built at

examples. By 1954 the Washingtons had given way to the revolutionary English Electric Canberra twin jet and the bulk of the fleet returned to the USAF. At Watton, 192 Squadron soldiered on with the type in the radio countermeasures role until February 1958.

The first Washington to arrive in Britain, WF437, had served the USAAF from Guam in the Pacific, initially named *Princess Pat*, later as *City of Trenton*. It had carried out

"The Washingtons provided a stopgap before the planned V-bombers entered service. Their appearance was fortuitous, five months later the Korean War broke out..."

**Left**
*Washington B.1 WF553 was issued to 15 Squadron at Coningsby on June 13, 1951. After several attempts to land in very bad weather at Coningsby on January 5, 1953, this aircraft hit the ground south of Horncastle. Five of the crew were killed, one was seriously injured five others scrambled from the wreckage unhurt.*
PETE WEST

35 perilous missions against Japan before being retired in the autumn of 1945. The rapidly changing political situation meant that 'Six-Eight-Zero' was reactivated, joining Strategic Air Command in 1948.

Earmarked for the RAF, the veteran was based at Marham for all of its service life. After the WCU, it transferred to 207 Squadron in July

1951 and joined 35 Squadron in December 1952. It was returned to the USA in 1953 and, like the bulk of the RAF's Washingtons, was scrapped, in 1954.

Among the dignitaries at the reception of the RAF's latest bomber was Maj General Leon W Johnson, commander of the USAF's Third Air Division. He was well versed

with Britain and the RAF, having commanded the Consolidated B-24 Liberator-equipped 44th Bombardment Group 'The Flying Eightballs' at Shipdham in 1943 and later the 14th Combat Bombardment Wing. He summed up the role of the Washingtons – and the V-Bombers to come – as follows: "They will never strike out, they will only strike back". ⊙

**Above left**
*Washington B.1 WF549 alongside another of the big Boeing bombers. This machine served at Marham as 'M-for-Mike' with both 90 Squadron (1951 to 1953) and 207 Squadron (1953 to 1954).*

**Above**
*Washington flight and ground crew members plus support vehicles in an official photograph at Coningsby in 1950.*

**Left**
*A trio of Washingtons of Marham-based 115 Squadron in December 1950. In the foreground is WF446 which served the unit from July 1950 to April 1953.*
ALL KEC

# ENGLISH ELECTRIC
# CANBERRA
## 1951 TO 2006

**Below**
*Close formation of B.2s of Wittering-based 100 Squadron, 1955.*
PETER GREEN COLLECTION

All eyes turned skyward. The personnel gathered witnessed a brief, impromptu flying display followed by a spirited beat-up of the airfield. After landing, test pilot Wg Cdr Roland Beamont got out and was greeted by the Station Commander, Gp Capt Sheen, and the Wingco Flying, Wg Cdr Connelly. The brand-new aircraft was signed over – Bomber Command had entered the jet age.

It was May 25, 1951 and Beamont had flown Canberra B.2 WD936 across the Pennines from its birthplace at Warton to Binbrook on the Lincolnshire Wolds, the home of 101 Squadron. Bomber Command was changing over from the stately four-engined, piston-powered Avro Lincoln and Boeing Washington to the sprightly twin-jet.

The story of the type's first ever delivery does not end with that anecdote. Two days later a letter from the Air Ministry landed, on Beamont's desk at Warton, expressing the displeasure of the 'Bomber Barons' at the manner in which the Canberra had arrived. Bombers were not expected to be flown in that fashion and, in future, were to be delivered *without* aerobatics!

The Canberra's bombload was modest despite its radically greater performance than its predecessors. With a crew of only three, it was set to cause a major change in the aircrew establishment. As a single-pilot bomber, there was a problem of conversion. The dual-control trainer T.4 was not due to enter service until mid-1953.

In the meantime, the Jet Conversion Unit (JCU) at Binbrook used Gloster Meteors for basic conversion and handling, together with Canberra B.2s for on-type instruction with an over-the-shoulder "watch what I do and then do it yourself" technique.

In early January 1952 administration of JCU was handed over to the next Canberra unit, 617 Squadron, its first aircraft (WD961) arriving on the 21st. As the numbers of aircraft increased and demand for crews grew, JCU gave way to 231 Operational Conversion Unit (OCU) in the latter part of 1951, at Bassingbourn. Eventually Canberra B.2s equipped 23 Bomber Command squadrons within Britain.

## TOSS-BOMBING

The basic Canberra B.2 had been a modified concept from the blind bomber/target-marker first specified, but work continued to fulfil the original specifications, including a crew of two. The development prototype, the one-off B.5 VX185, incorporated extra fuel uprated Rolls-Royce Avon 109s; but the radar bombing system was still not available, so the crew of three stayed. This variant went into production as the B.6 and began re-equipping units from June 1954, the first being 101 Squadron.

For use with the Near East and Far East Air Forces, the B.15 and B.16 versions of the B.6, respectively, were developed.

Canberras were in action in Malaya during Operation 'Firedog', countering communist insurgents. In October and November 1956, Canberras took part in the Suez conflict, units being based at Luqa on Malta and Nicosia on Cyprus.

For Bomber Command's deterrent role, it was soon realised that a more survivable technique was required for the delivery of nuclear weapons. In the early 1950s the USAF had perfected the Low Altitude Bombing System (LABS) and, in 1955, work was urgently progressing to introduce it to the RAF. This technique of low-level

"...the USAF had perfected the Low Altitude Bombing System... This technique of low-level penetration and 'toss-bombing' gave the Canberra a new lease of life."

## ENGLISH ELECTRIC CANBERRA B.2

| | |
|---|---|
| Type: | Three-crew light bomber |
| First flight: | May 13, 1949, entered service May 1951 |
| Powerplant: | Two 6,500lb st (28.91kN) Rolls-Royce Avon 101 turbojets |
| Dimensions: | Span 63ft 1⅛in (19.26m), Length 65ft 6in (19.96m) |
| Weights: | Empty 22,200lb (10,069kg), All-up 46,000lb (20,865kg) |
| Max speed: | 570mph (917km/h) at 40,000ft (12,192m) |
| Range: | 2,660 miles (4,280km) |
| Armament: | Up to 6,000lb (2,721kg) of bombs |
| Replaced: | Bomber variants only: Boeing Washington from 1905, Avro Lincoln from 1951, de Havilland Mosquito from 1952 |
| Taken on charge: | All RAF variants: 796, including sub-contracts to Avro, Handley Page and Short |
| Replaced by: | Bomber variants only: Vickers Valiant from 1956, Avro Vulcan and Handley Page from 1958 |

## VARIETY, LONGEVITY

And that is the briefest of summaries of the Canberra with Bomber Command. As with many types in this centenary tribute, two pages can only scratch the surface of the Canberra's RAF heritage. However, we shouldn't forget its incredible export success including licence production in Australia and its adoption by the USAF and built by Martin as the B-57 - an exceptional achievement.

From 1956 to 1971 the radically

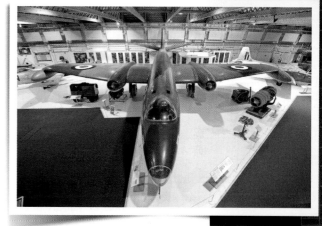

altered B(I).8 served five squadrons in West Germany. This featured a fighter-like canopy, offset to port, and a gun pack in the belly. The 'I' stood for Interdictor, but many RAF crews preferred the World War Two term 'Intruder'.

Canberras also served in the crew trainer, electronic countermeasures, target facilities and target-towing roles.

Like the Mosquito before it, the Canberra also excelled in photo-reconnaissance. The B.2-based PR.3 entered service in 1952 and it was joined by the PR.7, derived from the B.6, in 1954.

It was the big-winged, fighter-canopied, 11,250lb st (50.04kN) Avon 206-powered 'hot rod' PR.9 that took the Canberra into the 21st century. The last examples retired in July 2006, ending more than five decades of loyal and varied service.

penetration and 'toss-bombing' gave the Canberra a new lease of life. The B.6s of 9 Squadron at Binbrook were the first to be modified for LABS, returning to the unit in March 1958.

When 35 Squadron wound down at Upwood in September 1961, the B.2 left the front line and the two B.6 units followed suit in July 1961, thus ending the Canberra's service with Bomber Command.

# VICKERS
# VALIANT
## 1955 TO 1965

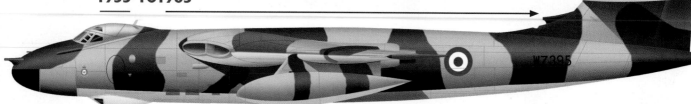

**V**ulcans raiding the Falklands are forever fixed in the minds of readers. However, it is as well to remember that the Valiant dropped bombs in anger 26 years before the Avro delta. The Valiant was the only V-bomber to release nuclear weapons – thankfully only for trial purposes.

As the political situation with Egypt decayed, following the nationalisation of the Suez Canal, Britain and France began to assemble an air and sea armada to regain control of the strategic asset.

A force of the RAF's latest bomber, the Valiant, from 138, 148, 207 and 214 Squadrons arrived at Luqa on Malta in late October 1956. Along with English Electric Canberras, the Valiants were tasked with destroying the Egyptian Air Force's (EAF) bases and other targets.

During the late afternoon of the last day of October 21 Valiants in four waves set off an on 1,800-mile (2,896km) round trip. The raid destined for Cairo West was called back soon after take-off when it was reported that American citizens were being evacuated from the airfield.

The remainder ploughed on, with Abu Sueir, Almaza and Kabrit as their objectives; each Valiant carried a dozen 1,000lb (453kg) bombs. A few aircraft, designated as 'pathfinders', carried 1,000-pounder target indicators and flare bundles in place of some of the conventional munitions.

Anti-aircraft fire was intense over the targets, but ineffectual at the Valiants' release height of 30,000ft (9,144m). One bomber was intercepted by an EAF Gloster Meteor night-fighter, but violent evasive action shook it off.

Over the nights of November 1/2, 2/3 and 4/5 Valiants carried out another five raids, all returning unscathed. Two of these involved striking at the large army camp at

Huckstep. By the end of this phase the EAF had effectively been neutralised. Amphibious landings followed, but the work of the Valiants was complete. On November 7 the Anglo-French forces were compelled to withdraw under pressure from the US and United Nations.

## FIRST OF THREE

Vickers was contracted to build the relatively low-risk Valiant as the first of the trio of V-bombers – Avro and Handley Page opting for radical aerodynamics for the Vulcan and Victor. The prototype was flown for the first time on May 18, 1951 and the initial operational unit was 138 Squadron at Gaydon in February 1955.

From the outset, the Valiant was to have roles beyond that of strategic bomber, with the capability of carrying comprehensive photo-reconnaissance equipment palettes, or in-flight refuelling equipment, in the bomb bay.

In 1961 the Valiant bomber force was re-profiled for low-level tactical nuclear strike. The last unit to fly the Vickers bomber in the strategic

role was 7 Squadron at Wittering, in September 1962. During 1964 the fleet was camouflaged, emphasizing the new tactic.

Designed to fly up to 54,000ft and not down at 5,000 or lower, the Valiant fleet was discovered to be suffering from stress loadings, and between December 1964 and February 1965 the entire fleet was withdrawn. Tanker specialist 214 Squadron at Marham was the last to give up the pioneering type.

The last-ever Valiant flight took place on April 23, 1968 when XD816, retained by Vickers for trials from Wisley, was ferried to Abingdon to take its place in the static at the 50th anniversary celebrations of the RAF. Afterwards it was scrapped on site.

## BIGGER BOMBS

First flown at Brooklands on September 4, 1956, XD818 had been selected as one of eight B.1s to try out Britain's nuclear arsenal. Extensive modifications were installed, including enhanced navigation and communications systems, data recording devices and screens, shutters and seals to increase

## VICKERS VALIANT B.1

| | |
|---|---|
| **Type:** | Five-crew heavy bomber |
| **First flight:** | May 18, 1951, entered service February 1955 |
| **Powerplant:** | Four 10,500lb st (46.7kN) Rolls-Royce Avon 204 turbojets |
| **Dimensions:** | Span 114ft 4in (34.84m), Length 108ft 3in (32.99m) |
| **Weights:** | Empty 75,881lb (34,419kg), All-up 140,000lb (63,504kg) |
| **Max speed:** | 414mph (666km/h) at sea level |
| **Range:** | 4,500 miles (7,241km) |
| **Armament:** | Up to 21,000lb (9,525kg) of bombs |
| **Replaced:** | English Electric Canberra from 1956 |
| **Taken on charge:** | 104 |
| **Replaced by:** | Handley Page Victor from 1958 |

fusion bomb codenamed 'Short Granite' at 11:38 hours local. The Valiant turned away in a carefully devised manoeuvre and about 150 seconds after release the crew, shrouded in darkness flying on instruments, felt very little turbulence as the shock wave billowed outwards.

This was the first-ever release of a nuclear weapon from a British aircraft. Hubbard and all of his crew received the Air Force Cross for their skills.

The intention was that Short Granite would unleash one megaton of explosive power but due to a 'trigger' problem, the yield turned out to be in the region of 0.3mt. This statistic

**Left**
*Receiver's eye view of a 214 Squadron Valiant tanker.*
FLIGHT REFUELLING

**Above**
*Valiant BK.1 XD818 is displayed within the National Cold War Exhibition at the RAF Museum Cosford. This aircraft took part in Operation 'Grapple' trials in May 1957; it was acquired by the museum in May 1965.*
RAF MUSEUM
www.rafmuseum.org

**Left**
*Line-up of Valiants at 232 Operational Conversion Unit, Gaydon, summer 1955. To the left are Canberra T.4s.* KEC

**Below left**
*Newly camouflaged Valiant BK.1 XD821 of 232 Operational Conversion Unit in the summer of 1964. Built in 1956, it was retired in November 1964.*
KEC-ROY BONSER

## "Anti-aircraft fire was intense over the targets... One bomber was intercepted by an Egyptian Gloster Meteor night-fighter, but violent evasive action shook it off."

crew survivability after detonation.

After flight trials XD818 was delivered to Wittering for 49 Squadron, under the command of Wg Cdr Kenneth Hubbard. On March 3, 1957, with Hubbard as captain, the aircraft set out westwards across the Atlantic and North America via Honolulu, Hawaii, to the British territory of Christmas Island, 300 miles (482km) south of the coast of Java, Indonesia.

Four 49 Squadron Valiants were to take part in Operation 'Grapple', Britain's nuclear weapon trials. Drops were to take place adjacent to an atoll 400 miles southwest of Christmas Island with the weapons set to air-burst. Training got under way with the release of 100lb (45kg) conventional practice bombs to determine the margin of error, followed by 10,000lb high-explosive bombs.

Captained by Hubbard, co-piloted by Fg Off R L Beeson, XD818 climbed to 35,000ft (10,668m) on May 15 and released a thermonuclear

caused politicians a lot of grief as the trials were meant to show that the UK was in the 'big league'.

Two more 'nukes' were dropped during Grapple, on May 31 and June 19. The Valiants returned to Christmas Island for Grapples 'X' (November to December 1957), 'Y' (March to April 1958) and 'Z' (July to September 1958). The fifth drop took place on April 28, 1958 with Sqn Ldr R M Bates at the helm of XD825 when a 'Blue Danube' bomb achieved a strategically-satisfying yield of 3mt. Today Valiant XD818 is displayed at the RAF Museum Cosford. ◎

# AVRO
# VULCAN

## 1957 TO 1984

Vulcans have taken part in many overseas trips on 'flag waving' sorties or long-ranging exercises, but the visit of XM597 to Galeas Air Base, Rio de Janeiro, Brazil, on June 2, 1982 was by far the most momentous, hitting the headlines the world over.

Vulcans, pooled under the aegis of Waddington-based 44 Squadron, Vulcans and Handley Page Victor K.2 tankers gathered at Wideawake airfield, Ascension Island, in May 1982 to take part in ultra-long bombing raids as part of Operation 'Corporate', the liberation of the Falklands Islands.

For *Black Buck 4* – the raid of 28/29th May 28/29 – XM597 was slotted as the 'Primary' with XM598 as the reserve. Argentinian radar sites around Port Stanley were the target, with both of the Vulcan's underwing pylons toting 'twin-packs' of AGM-54A Shrike anti-radiation missiles.

The crew for XM597 comprised the captain, Sqn Ldr Neil McDougall; co-pilot Fg Off Chris Lackham; radar nav plotter Flt Lt Dave Castle; nav plotter Flt Lt Barry Smith; air electronics officer (AEO) Flt Lt Rod Trevaskus; and air-to-air refuelling instructor (AARI) Flt Lt Brian Gardner.

The AARI was from the Victor tanker force and swapped with the co-pilot when a top-up was due, advising and guiding the captain as Vulcan crews had long since stopped training on in-flight refuelling (IFR). *Black Buck 4* aborted, however, when a Victor K.2 went unserviceable while the entire 'circus' was a long way towards the tiny South Atlantic target.

The whole raid – same crews, same aircraft – was rescheduled as *Black Buck 5* for the night of May 30/31. Arrival in the target area was to coincide with an HS Harrier strike so that the Argentinians would be forced to use their radar, enabling *Black Buck 5*'s AEO to get a 'fix' so that the Shrikes could do their work. Three AGM-54As were launched, but damage assessment could not be undertaken.

The same combo of crew and aircraft assembled for the night of June 2/3 as *Black Buck 6*, another four-up Shrike mission – but this time with a low-level profile followed by a sharp pull-up in the hope of tempting the radar stations to 'illuminate' the delta. Two Shrikes were fired and it's thought one damaged the principal radar site.

## WITHOUT A HOPE

The hook-up with the first of several Victors after the raid ended in disaster: the IFR probe fractured. Without a hope of continuing to the next tanker, XM597 set course for Rio de Janeiro, the only possible diversion airfield that didn't involve Argentina.

Naturally it would have been better for the Brazilians if the aircraft were not armed, so the remaining Shrikes were jettisoned. One refused to go and caused many diplomatic red faces when *Black Buck 6* landed at Galeas with virtually dry tanks – probably not enough for a 'go-around'.

Crew and aircraft were 'held' for a week then released – minus the errant missile and on the strict proviso that XM597 was not to be used on operations again. For this Vulcan the war was over! It arrived at Ascension on June 10 and was back at Waddington 72 hours later.

When the *Black Buck* raids were staged, the Vulcan was in its twilight years with the RAF, and on April 12, 1984 the V-bomber at the centre

of a diplomatic incident was ferried north to its new home at the National Museum of Flight Scotland at East Fortune, east of Edinburgh.

## MIGHTY DELTA

Knowledge of how delta wings behaved was very basic when the Vulcan was conceived and, unsurprisingly, when the prototype took its maiden flight on August 30, 1952 it was the largest aircraft to employ that planform.

The design offered great speed, a huge bomb bay with minimal centre of gravity problems and – as established in early flights – aerobatic performance.

The first frontline unit to take on the mighty delta was 83 Squadron at Waddington in July 1957. As the first of the 45 B.1s ordered were being manufactured, Avro was already

at work on the much more powerful B.2 which, with a bigger wing, was to carry the Blue Steel nuclear standoff missile.

The prototype B.2 first flew on August 31, 1957, and again it was 83 Squadron that brought the new version into service. The Blue Steel was declared operation with 617 Squadron, at Scampton, in February 1963 but it had only a short service life.

The following year the fleet took on camouflage and in 1966 adopted a low-level penetration profile, aided by General Dynamics terrain-following radar. On April 30, 1968 Bomber Command became part of the new Strike Command in readiness for the Royal Navy taking over the national nuclear deterrent role in June 1969 as Polaris-armed submarines came on line.

In anticipation of being equipped with the later cancelled Douglas Skybolt nuclear missile, some Vulcan B.2s had been 'plumbed in' with hardpoints under each wing, which were used on a small number of B.2MRR (occasionally called SR.2) versions for maritime reconnaissance and air sampling by 27 Squadron from November 1973 to March 1982.

The hardpoints came into their own during the Falklands conflict to carry Shrike missiles, as shown above, the war providing a stunning finale for the Vulcan in the bomber role before 44 Squadron disbanded in December 1982.

The aftermath found the RAF in need of in-flight refuelling assets, and the stopgap Vulcan K.2 tanker version served with 50 Squadron from Waddington until March 1984. With that, the type's operational career came to a close. ◉

## AVRO VULCAN B.2

| | |
|---|---|
| **Type:** | Five-crew heavy bomber |
| **First flight:** | August 30,1952; B.1 entered service July 1957 |
| **Powerplant:** | Four 20,000lb st (89.6kN) Bristol Siddeley Olympus 301 turbojets |
| **Dimensions:** | Span 111ft 0in (33.83m), Length 99ft 11in (30.45m) |
| **Weights:** | All-up about 250,000lb (113,400kg) |
| **Max speed:** | 645mph (1,037km/h) at 36,000ft (10,972m) |
| **Range:** | 4,600 miles (7,403km) |
| **Armament:** | Up to 21,000lb (9,525kg) of bombs; or Blue Steel nuclear standoff weapon |
| **Replaced:** | English Electric Canberra from 1957 |
| **Taken on charge:** | 134 |
| **Replaced by:** | Hawker Siddeley Buccaneer from 1969; Panavia Tornado from 1983 |

# HANDLEY PAGE
# VICTOR

## 1958 TO 1993

**Above**
*Built as a B.2 in 1962, XL512 was converted to a K.2 in 1976. During the last days of Lightning operational flying, it tanked F.6 XR728 in May 1988 for the benefit of the press. The Victor was scrapped in 1994; the Lightning lives on, preserved at Bruntingthorpe.*
KEY-DUNCAN CUBITT

Faster, higher, further, greater weapon load, longer life, veteran of *two* wars. These, and others, are the attributes the Victor holds over its comrade the Vulcan. Yet it is always the delta-winged V-bombers that gets the plaudits.

The Victor programme did not have a good start. The prototype, which first flew on Christmas Eve 1952, suffered a structural failure on July 14, 1954, killing all four on board. The second example, WB775, entered flight test on September 11 that year and Handley Page went all out to return some pace to the programme.

The first production B.1, XA917, had its maiden flight on January 30, 1956. Mk.1s were powered by 11,050lb st (49.15kN) Armstrong Siddeley Sapphire 200 series turbojets.

The following year, XA917 hit the headlines, for good reasons. John Allam was flying a routine sortie testing the longitudinal stability and the Victor entered a shallow dive. The signature double boom of the 'sound barrier' being broken was heard over a wide area.

Handley Page put out a press release the following week, keen to make the most of its supersonic V-bomber and score more than a few points over its rival, Avro. John was quoted as having had his attention diverted momentarily at above 40,000ft (12,192m) when he noticed the Mach meter had reached the magic '1' with a true airspeed of about

675mph (1,086km/h). He said that it: "behaved in its customary stable manner".

Victor XA917 was the largest aircraft at the time to have gone supersonic and much was made of flight test observer Paul Langston, seated in the navigator's position, as the first man to travel at Mach one *backwards*!

John and Frank 'Spud' Murphy demonstrated the eighth production Victor B.1, XA930, at the 1958 Farnborough airshow in September 1958. The pair had been perfecting rolls off the top to highlight the big aircraft's agility. The first operational B.1 unit was 10 Squadron at Cottesmore in January 1958.

## HANDLEY PAGE VICTOR B.2

| | |
|---|---|
| **Type:** | Five-crew heavy bomber |
| **First flight:** | December 24, 1952, B.1 entered service January 1958 |
| **Powerplant:** | Four 19,750lb st (87.84kN) Rolls-Royce Conway 201 turbofans |
| **Dimensions:** | Span 120ft 0in (36.57m), Length 114ft 11in (35.02m) |
| **Weights:** | Empty 114,240lb (51,819kg), All-up 223,000lb (101,152kg) |
| **Max speed:** | 647mph (1,041km/h) at 40,000ft (12,192m) |
| **Range:** | 3,500 miles (5,632km) |
| **Armament:** | Up to 35,000lb (15,876kg) of bombs, or a Blue Steel nuclear stand-off weapon |
| **Replaced:** | Vickers Valiant from 1958 |
| **Taken on charge:** | 84 |
| **Replaced by:** | In tanker role: Vickers VC-10 from 1984 and Lockheed Tristar from 1986 |

## TANKER SUPREME

Mk.1s underwent a change of role as the Valiant tanker force had been phased out by early 1965. The Victor's incredible lifting capability, 35,000lb (15,876kg), made it a perfect 'flying petrol station'. Two-hose Victor tankers began to appear in mid-1965, shortly followed by three-pointers. In July 1966 the two tanker units, 55 and 57 Squadrons, were joined by the re-formed 214 Squadron, also at Marham, and the Victor dropped the bomber role.

With the B.2, the Victor evolved considerably and traded the Sapphires for Rolls-Royce Conway turbofans, a bigger wing, enhanced

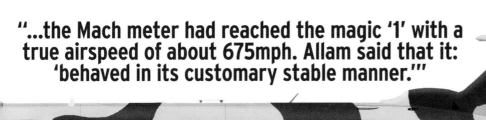

"...the Mach meter had reached the magic '1' with a true airspeed of about 675mph. Allam said that it: 'behaved in its customary stable manner.'"

aerodynamics and even greater performance. At Wittering, 139 Squadron became the first to use B.2s from February 1962, adopting the Blue Steel stand-off missile the following year. Defence cuts reduced the planned fleet to 34 and they were put through an engine upgrade programme in 1964.

The highly capable SR.2 strategic reconnaissance conversion started operations in May 1965 with 543 Squadron at Wyton. The globetrotters at 543 carried out their demanding tasks until the unit disbanded in May 1974.

Handley Page went into liquidation on August 8, 1969, overstretched by the ambitious and problematic Jetstream twin-turboprop programme. A rescue plan was put into effect but on February 27, 1970 one of the most famous names in the British aviation threw in the towel.

Parked all over the Handley Page airfield at Radlett were B.2s awaiting conversion to K.2s tankers. These were ferried to Woodford where Hawker Siddeley took over the project and the first conversion began flight testing in March 1972.

On May 7, 1974 K.2 XL233 was delivered to 232 Operational Conversion Unit at Marham and 55 Squadron adopted the type in July 1975, to be followed by 57 Squadron. Across the ramp, 214 Squadron disbanded in January 1977 and the last of the Mk.1 tankers were retired.

During April 1982 the bulk of 55 and 57 Squadron's K.2s were shoehorned into crowded Wideawake airfield on the Ascension Islands as the RAF got ready to support the Royal Navy task force to liberate the Falkland Islands from Argentine occupation. Page 96 has highlighted one of the famous *Black Buck* sorties – the longest bombing raids ever undertaken by the RAF.

The Vulcan aircrew involved were the first to lay praise on the Victor tanker teams. Putting a single Vulcan over Port Stanley involved pinpoint timing from *eleven* leap-frogging Victor K.2s as they topped up the delta-winged bomber on their way into the South Atlantic. Another four of the tankers were needed as the 'reception committee' to bring the Vulcan back to Wideawake.

Victors were also tasked with very long-range reconnaissance and signals intelligence sorties as well as tanking other RAF assets, including

Hawker Siddeley Nimrods. Back at Marham, the remainder of the fleet were working hard helping maintain the air bridge to and from Wideawake while continuing to meet RAF commitments in Europe.

War was again on the agenda when Iraq invaded Kuwait, and coalition forces began to gather in the Middle East prior to the brief and brutal Operation 'Desert Storm' – in RAF parlance Operation 'Granby' – of January and February 1991. The first four K.2s – 55 Squadron then the only frontline operator of the type – deployed to Muharraq, Bahrain, on December 14, 1990. By the time the shooting started – on the night of January 16 – there were eight Victors at readiness.

Like the Buccaneers and Tornados – pages 90 and 92 – most of the Victors gained American-style nose-art and names: XH671 *Slinky Sue*, XH672 *Maid Marion*, XL164 *Saucy Sal*, XL231 *Lusty Lindy*, XM715 *Teasin' Tina* and XM717 *Lucky Lou* – XL161 and XL190 declined the attention of the artists.

The Victors conducted 299 combat tanker sorties in 870 flying hours with 'clients' including US Navy fighters as well as RAF types. On October 15, 1993 a ceremony at Marham marked the disbanding of 55 Squadron, in-flight refuelling becoming the domain of converted airliners, Lockheed Tristars and Vickers VC-10s. ◎

**Top**
*Victor K.2 XM715 of 55 Squadron, Marham, 1975. This machine became a Falklands and First Gulf War veteran and is today preserved 'in steam' at Bruntingthorpe.*
PETE WEST

**Above**
*On November 30, 1993 K.2 XH672 of 55 Squadron touched down at Shawbury ready for transportation by road to the nearby RAF Museum Cosford. This was the last ever flight by a Victor. Converted to a tanker in 1974, XH672 had the highest sortie rate during the Falklands conflict and flew 52 'ops' during the First Gulf War.*
RAF MUSEUM
www.rafmuseum.org

**Left**
*The spacious flight deck and exceptional view of a 55 Squadron K.2.* KEY-DUNCAN CUBITT

# HAWKER SIDDELEY
# BUCCANEER

## 1969 TO 1994

XT275

**Above**
*Buccaneer S.2B XT275 of 208 Squadron, Honington, 1980. It was built for the Fleet Air Arm and entered service with 801 Squadron in 1965, transferring the RAF in 1977 and retiring in 1985.*
© ANDY HAY WWW.flyingart.co.uk

**Right**
*Impressive line-up at Lossiemouth on April 30, 1988 to celebrate the 30th anniversary of the first flight of the prototype Buccaneer. Included are aircraft from 12 and 208 Squadron and 237 Operational Conversion Unit.*
RAF LOSSIEMOUTH

While touring the Buccaneer production line at Brough on Humberside in mid-1976  the last six aircraft were nearing completion  the author was struck by a cartoon pinned to a work station. It was alongside a 'girlie calendar'  they were an obligatory management accessory in those days  and the first 'frame' showed an enormous ingot being delivered to the factory.

The second drawing depicted several of these giant blocks, each one being 'attacked' by men with hammers and chisels. The final image was of a pristine, gleaming Buccaneer surrounded be large chunks of discarded metal. The message was that Buccaneers were so strong because they weren't assembled – they were sculpted from solid metal. (This was based on fact; elements of the Buccaneer's airframe were, indeed, milled from ingots.)

Not far away at the flight test airfield, Holme-on-Spalding-Moor, inside the flight shed was a banner also alluding to the durability of the jet, but with a helping of Yorkshire self-deprecation: 'Buccaneer  Honed to Perfection and Hammered to Fit'.

The Buccaneer had an illustrious career with the RAF, but from its selection it suffered from the 'not invented here' syndrome. This machine was an upstart, the RAF was adopting an aircraft that had been designed for, and operated by, the Royal Navy.

### NOWHERE TO GO

Designed to meet an exacting requirement for the Fleet Air Arm, the prototype Buccaneer first flew on April 30, 1958. The navy wanted

**"With nowhere else to turn, the RAF finally focussed on the Buccaneer. Few realised at the time, but it turned out to be the last all-British bomber to serve the RAF."**

a low-level, high-speed, nuclear-capable, carrier-borne strike aircraft. To achieve this Blackburn used advanced aerodynamics, boundary layer control to keep approach speeds reasonable, advanced electronics for the low-level environment and a rotating bomb door to keep the airframe 'clean'.

The initial version, the S.1 was powered by a pair of 7,100lb st (31.58kN) de Havilland Gyron Junior 101 turbojets. The first frontline unit was 801 Squadron, taking its first examples in July 1962 and embarking them on HMS *Ark Royal* in February 1963. In the same year Blackburn became part of Hawker Siddeley.

Much more powerful Rolls-Royce Spey turbofans were fitted to the further refined S.2, the prototype having its maiden flight on May 17, 1963. This version entered service with 801 Squadron at Lossiemouth in October 1965. With the scrapping of the Royal Navy's 'big' aircraft carriers in 1978, the Fleet Air Arm retired its Buccaneers.

Aware of the Buccaneer as it was being developed, the RAF shunned it in favour of the BAC TSR.2 but the programme was cancelled in 1965. In the void created by the TSR.2, the American General Dynamics F-111K 'swing-wing' strike aircraft was ordered, only for this to fall by the wayside in 1968.

With nowhere else to turn, the RAF finally focussed on the

Buccaneer. Few realised at the time, but it turned out to be the last all-British bomber to serve the RAF.

Surplus Royal Navy stocks were joined by 49 examples ordered from new. Production was completed in October 1977 when XZ432 was delivered to 15 Squadron at Lossiemouth. The first Buccaneer S.2Bs were issued to 12 Squadron at Honington in October 1969.

Initially, Buccaneers were used in West Germany for low-level nuclear strike and in Britain for maritime strike. With the advent of the Tornado, Buccaneer units were concentrated at Lossiemouth in anti-shipping and precision strike roles.

## BRIDGE BUSTERS

Skills acquired with laser designation pods and laser-guided bombs (LGBs), plus the Buccaneer's prowess at low-level meant that a detachment was sent to Muharraq, Bahrain, in readiness for the

liberation of Kuwait from the Iraqi armed forces. The first aircraft arrived on January 26, 1991.

Initially the Buccaneers were used to designate targets for the Tornado force, but soon were dropping 1,000-pounder LGBs of their

own. Buccaneers made possible the destruction of the bridge at As Samawah across the Euphrates, north west of Basra, on February 2, 1991. This success led to two dozen more bridges being downed before the Buccaneers specialised in blowing holes in hardened aircraft shelters at airfields.

Buccaneers completed 216 'ops' during the First Gulf War. After return to Lossiemouth, the wind down was swift, 12 Squadron retiring the type in October 1993 and 208 Squadron said farewell in April 1994.

Despite its almost reluctant acceptance by the RAF, the Buccaneer earned the admiration of aircrew and high command alike. As the Gulf War demonstrated, it was a very capable machine and the king of low-level flying. An aircrew member paid tribute by saying that riding down on the deck in a Buccaneer was "like a ball bearing on glass." ⊙

### HAWKER SIDDELEY BUCCANEER S.2B

| Type: | Two-seat low-level strike |
|---|---|
| First flight: | April 30, 1958, entered service October 1969 |
| Powerplant: | Two 11,200lb st (45.81kN) Rolls-Royce Spey 101 turbofans |
| Dimensions: | Span 44ft 0in (13.41m), Length 63ft 5in (19.32m) |
| Weights: | Empty 29,980lb (13,598kg), All-up 62,000lb (28,123kg) |
| Max speed: | 645mph (1,037km/h) at sea level |
| Range: | 700 miles (1,126km) |
| Armament: | Up to 16,000lb (7,256kg) of bombs and missiles, in rotary bomb bay and on under-wing pylons |
| Replaced: | Avro Vulcan from 1969, English Electric Canberra B(I).8 from 1972 |
| Taken on charge: | 49 newly built, 62 transferred from the Fleet Air Arm |
| Replaced by: | Panavia Tornado from 1982 |

**Above left**
*Lossiemouth Buccaneer S.2Bs in their element, low-level and over water, in the mid-1980s. In the foreground is XN981 of 12 Squadron which served with the Fleet Air Arm from 1965, transferring to the RAF initially in 1970, and permanently from 1978. It carries a Martel anti-ship missile and an electronic countermeasures pod under its port wing. In the background is XZ432, the last Buccaneer built, delivered to the RAF on October 6, 1977.*
BRITISH AEROSPACE

**Above**
*A Buccaneer outside a hardened aircraft shelter at Lossiemouth, showing off armament options.*

**Above left**
*The RAF Museum's Buccaneer S.2B XW547 was acquired in January 1993 and is displayed at Hendon. It wears the colours and nose-art worn during the First Gulf War, during which it successfully completed 11 sorties.*
RAF MUSEUM
www.rafmuseum.org

# PANAVIA TORNADO

## 1981 TO PRESENT

**Right**
*A Tornado GR.1 of Laarbruch-based 20 Squadron in Gulf War 'pink' colours with a pair of ALARM anti-radiation missiles under the centre section and a pair of 465-gallon 'Hindenburg' long-range tanks on the inner wing pylons.*
GEOFF LEE - BRITISH AEROSPACE

**Below right**
*Cockpit of a Tornado GR.1.*
BRITISH AEROSPACE

There is a strong argument that the Tornado is the most significant warplane the RAF has operated since World War Two – perhaps of all time. Since the First Gulf War of 1991 the Tornado force has been almost constantly on call, acting as what the RAF calls "a rapid and flexible crisis response tool".

From the middle of this year the Marham Tornado units, 9, 12 and 31 Squadrons, will begin to wind down as the Lockheed Martin F-35B begins to gear up and replace the venerable 'swing-wing' jets. It is intended that the final Tornados will be paid off in 2019, having completed nearly four decades of service, more than half of that in combat situations.

The BAC/Sud Concorde supersonic transport proved that multi-nation production programmes were possible and led to the very successful Anglo-French SEPECAT Jaguar strike fighter. Beyond this Britain, Germany and Italy pooled resources and formed the Panavia conglomerate to develop the Multi-Role Combat Aircraft, which gelled as the Tornado.

The prototype was flown at Manching in West Germany on August 14, 1974 followed by the British prototype at Warton, 78 days later. As noted below, the first deliveries in the UK were in July 1980 to a groundbreaking, multi-national establishment.

The first operational RAF unit was 9 Squadron at Honington, which received its GR.1s from January 1982. With the withdrawal of the maritime strike Hawker Siddeley Buccaneers in 1983, the GR.1B was introduced, equipped with Sea Eagle anti-surface vessel missiles.

The fleet has constantly received upgrades, the most significant being the greatly enhanced GR4. The prototype conversion, XZ631, flew on May 29, 1993 and the first example was handed over for service in October 1997. (The RAF altered its long-held designation system in 2008,

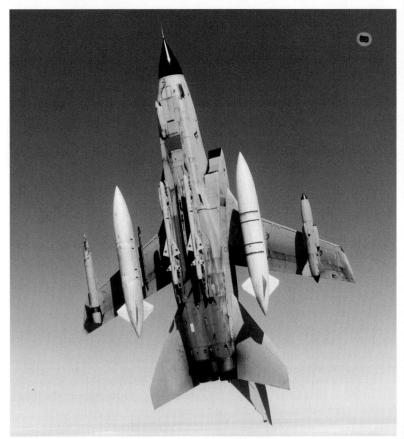

by removing full stops, hence GR4, not GR.4.)

Developed solely for the RAF was the Tornado ADV – air defence variant – stand-off interceptor that served from 1984 to 2011. It is described in the sister publication *RAF Centenary Celebration Fighters*.

### TRI-NATIONAL
Just as the entire Tornado programme benefited from the economies of scale, so it was decided the initial conversion training for pilots would be undertaken by a single, multi-national, unit. This was the Tri-National Tornado Training Establishment (TTTE) at Cottesmore, which took its first aircraft in July 1980.

Officially inaugurated on January 29, 1981 TTTE was completely integrated, aircraft flew from the

> "Tornados flew more than 1,500 'ops' during the campaign of January and February 1991. Four aircraft were lost to surface-to-air missiles or anti-aircraft artillery and three aircrew were killed."

base carrying RAF, Luftwaffe and Aeronautica Militare Italiana markings. Daily a British instructor could be training an Italian pilot in a German-owned aircraft, or any other combination. This also applied to maintenance and ground school personnel at Cottesmore.

Beyond TTTE, the three nations handled their own specialist routes to operational squadrons. For example, after Cottesmore RAF Tornado aircrew moved to the Tornado Weapons Conversion Unit (TWCU)

## PANAVIA TORNADO GR4

| Type: | Two-seat tactical strike/reconnaissance |
|---|---|
| First flight: | British prototype October 30, 1974, entered service October 1983 |
| Powerplant: | Two 16,000lb st (71.5kN) Turbo-Union RB.199 Mk.103 turbofans |
| Dimensions: | Span 45ft 7¾in (13.91m) unswept, 28ft 1in (8.56m) fully swept, Length 56ft 6in (17.23m) |
| Weights: | All-up 61,600lb (27,950kg) |
| Max speed: | 1,452mph (2,336km/h) at 36,000ft (10,972m) |
| Armament: | Up to 19,840lb (9,000kg) of ordnance, including Paveway II, III and IV series GPS/laser-guided bombs, Brimstone air-to-ground missiles, Storm Shadow cruise missiles, ASRAAM air-to-air missiles, plus internal 27mm Mauser cannon. |
| Replaced: | HS Buccaneer from 1983; SEPECAT Jaguar from 1985 |
| Taken on charge: | 228 |
| Replaced by: | Lockheed Georgia F-35B, scheduled from 2018 |

at Honington from August 1981. The role of TWCU was absorbed into 15 Squadron from April 1992.

Fleet sizes contracted in the mid-1990s and the TTTE closed, with each nation taking responsibility for Tornado aircrew training within their own boundaries. A ceremony was held at Cottesmore on March 31, 1999 to disband TTTE, bringing to an end a unique RAF unit.

### WAGING PEACE

A large force of Tornados began to assemble at Muharraq in Bahrain, and Dhahran and Tabuk in Saudi Arabia from late August 1990 as the United

Nations-mandated coalition began to build in response to the Iraqi invasion of Kuwait. RAF Tornados were in the thick of the combat, which was known as Operation 'Granby' in the RAF and 'Desert Storm' across the allies, in the precision strike and missile site suppression roles.

Tornados flew more than 1,500 'ops' during the short campaign of January and February 1991. Four aircraft were lost to surface-to-air missiles or anti-aircraft artillery and three aircrew were killed. Beyond Granby, Tornados were involved in no-fly zone policing of Iraqi airspace.

With the fall of the twin towers in

New York on September 11, 2001 the nature of military operations changed irreversibly. RAF Tornados were deployed to Afghanistan in 2009, replacing Harriers in Operation 'Herrick'. It was late 2014 when RAF strike assets were removed from Afghanistan.

Between March 20 and April 3, 2003 coalition forces were again at war with Iraq, this time toppling the Hussein regime. During Operation 'Telic', the Second Gulf War, Tornados took part in 1,353 combat sorties. The Tornado force was involved in strikes within Iraq against insurgent forces until May 2009 when the last mission was flown. Sadly, Tornados were not done with Iraqi airspace.

Eyes turned to Libya in November 2011 and Operation 'Ellamy'. Armed with Storm Shadow air-launched cruise missiles, Marham-based Tornados undertook a series of 3,000-mile (4,827km) round trips, tanked by Vickers VC-10s or Lockheed Tristars. Other missions were staged from Gioia de Colle in Italy.

From 2014 Tornados based at Akrotiri on Cyprus, along with Eurofighter Typhoon FGR4s, have been involved in countering the threat of Daesh, the so-called Islamic State, insurgency in Iraq and Syria. This is Operation 'Shader', which at the time of writing was on-going and likely to keep the Tornado in harm's way until the retirement of this exceptional warplane. ◎

# BAe/McDD
# HARRIER GR.5 TO 9
## 1988 TO 2010

**Right**
*A pair of 1 Squadron Harrier GR.5s on the ramp at Wittering. The aircraft in the background, ZD351, was built in 1988 and went through the upgrade programme all the way to GR.9A status in 2010.*
BRITISH AEROSPACE

E ven the weather was dismal on December 15, 2010 as the RAF paid off the incredible Harrier. The Joint Force Harrier was no more; its impending demise announced weeks earlier on October 12 under the Strategic Defence and Security Review. Most of the fleet were transferred to Arizona for spares consumption by the US Marine Corps.

Since the 'big-wing' GR.5, the Harrier had been a combined programme with McDonnell Douglas of the USA. The two talents had created an awesome strike weapon, which evolved to its final UK iteration, the GR.9A.

With the 'jump jet's' success, British Aerospace and McDonnell Douglas worked to create a second-generation version, initially for the US Marines Corps, as the AV-8B Harrier II. While maintaining the overall format of its forebears, this machine was significantly different with a new, larger wing. Nearly 30% of the airframe was of composite construction, the cockpit was enlarged and there were seven weapons stations. The prototype AV-8B had its maiden flight in November 1978.

Development for the RAF did not begin until the early 1980s and it was April 30, 1985 before the first GR.5 flew. In July 1969 the honour of introducing the world's first operational V/STOL fighter was

granted to 1 Squadron at Wittering. It was appropriate that the unit, still at Wittering, also inaugurated the second-generation Harrier, taking its first examples in November 1988.

The Mk.5 was impressive but advances in technology meant there was much more that the Anglo-American team could do. The result was the GR.7, a huge advance in capability from the GR.5 and a world apart from the somewhat basic GR.1s of 1969. (The early Harriers are covered in our sister publication, *RAF Centenary Celebration Fighters*.)

With the GR.7 the Harrier became a

true 'night bird', with forward-looking infrared and night-vision goggles to allow the pilot to carry out sorties in the worst of weather, and in darkness.

The prototype Mk.7 first appeared in 1990. As well as new-build examples, GR.5s were also upgraded to the new status. A two-seat conversion trainer with combat potential based on the GR.7 – the T.10 – was also produced. The first GR.7s were issued to 4 Squadron at Gütersloh, Germany, in September 1990.

The ultimate upgrade, the GR.9, entered service in October 2006. With the closure of Dunsfold, the prototype had its first flight from Warton, on May 30, 2003. The Fleet

Air Arm gave up its Sea Harrier FA.2s in March 2006 and the GR.9 fleet was pooled into Joint Force Harrier, based at Cottesmore, before falling victim to the 2010 defence review.

## MUSEUM PIECE
Bedecked with special markings to celebrate the Harrier's service life, 1969 to 2010, the RAF Museum's GR.9A ZG477 is one of the youngest exhibits at Cosford and never ceases to draw the attention of visitors. It was picked for display not just for its unique colours, but because its RAF career was so representative of the

## BRITISH AEROSPACE/
## MCDONNELL DOUGLAS HARRIER GR.7

| | |
|---|---|
| **Type:** | Single-seat V/STOL strike/reconnaissance |
| **First flight:** | GR.5: April 30, 1985, entered service March 1989 |
| **Powerplant:** | One 21,750lb st (96.74kN) Bristol Siddeley Pegasus 107 vectored-thrust turbofan |
| **Dimensions:** | Span 30ft 4in (9.25m), Length 46ft 4in (14.12m) |
| **Weights:** | Empty 12,500lb (5,700kg), All-up, conventional take-off 31,000lb (8,595kg) |
| **Max speed:** | 662mph (1m065km/h) |
| **Range:** | 300 miles (556km) |
| **Armament:** | Two 25mm ADEN cannon. Up to 8,000lb (3,650kg) of bombs, rockets |
| **Replaced:** | Hawker Siddeley Harrier GR.3 from 1988 |
| **Taken on charge:** | 96 – 62 new-build GR.5/GR.5A and 34 new-build GR.7 |
| **Replaced by:** | Taskings absorbed into the Tornado force 2010 |

## "...ZG477 was deployed to Kandahar, Afghanistan, as part of Operation 'Herrick'. A round-the-clock readiness was maintained for strikes using laser- or GPS-guided weapons, or tactical recce sorties."

second-generation Harriers. As such, its story provides a great insight into the operations of this sophisticated warplane.

It was built as a GR.7 and first flew at Dunsfold on September 3, 1990 before being taken on charge by the RAF two days later. Serving initially with 4 Squadron at Gütersloh, for just a few days ZG477 was based in *West* Germany as the country reunited on October 3. It transferred to 3 Squadron at Laarbruch in 1992, but by the following spring had returned to 4 Squadron.

During 1993 and 1994 the RAF Harrier units, 1, 3 and 4 Squadrons provided crews and aircraft at Incirlik, Turkey, policing the 'no-fly' zone of northern Iraqi airspace under Operation 'Warden'.

From the spring of 1999 the force was required for the interminably complex and woefully brutal politics of the Balkans and deployed to Gioia del Colle in the 'heel' of Italy as part of Operation 'Allied Force'. Harriers, including ZG477, were tasked to fly across the Adriatic Sea against Serbian forces during the Yugoslav civil war until the campaign wound down in late June 1999.

On April 1, 2000 Joint Force Harrier, the combined Fleet Air Arm and RAF operation of GR.7s and GR.9s was established at Cottesmore. By 2003 ZG477 had been upgraded to GR.7A status; the following year it became a GR.9A. During its time at Cottesmore, ZG477 flew with 3 Squadron, the Naval Strike Wing, 4 and finally 1 Squadron.

From June 2008 ZG477 was deployed to Kandahar, Afghanistan, as part of Operation 'Herrick'. A round-the-clock readiness was maintained for strikes using laser- or GPS-guided weapons, or tactical recce sorties.

The Harriers were back at Cottesmore in July 2009 and in November of the next year ZG477 was transferred to 1 Squadron – the very first frontline Harrier unit – to take part in the retirement ceremonies. On November 19, ZG477 was deployed with three others on HMS *Ark Royal* – also facing the axe – for its final cruise. Five days later, ZG477, flown by Lt Cdr James Blackmore, was the last to depart from the vessel's ski-jump.

On the very last day, December 15, ZG477 was part of a 16-aircraft final 'thrash' around former bases. After that, it was placed in 'overseen' storage at Cottesmore and, while ground-run, in the end it was not flown again. It made the road journey to Cosford on December 19, 2011. ◉

**Above**
*A Sidewinder air-to-air missile and rocket pod-equipped GR.7 of 232 Operational Conversion Unit, Wittering, 1992.*

**Left**
*GR.9A ZG477 in commemorative 1 Squadron colours at the RAF Museum, Cosford.*
RAF MUSEUM WWW. rafmuseum.org

**Below**
*Harrier GR.9 ZD328 of 41 Squadron – the Fast Jet and Weapons Operational Evaluation Unit – Coningsby, 2004.*
© ANDY HAY
www.flyingart.co.uk

# LOCKHEED MARTIN
# LIGHTNING II

## FROM 2018

Unlike every other aircraft profiled in this publication, the Lightning II has not entered operational service and, apart from airshow appearances in 2016, has yet to be based in the UK. With a unit cost of around £122 million each, nine examples are expected to be delivered to Marham by the middle of this year.

In hot competition with Boeing, Lockheed Martin was the winner of the American Joint Strike Fighter (JSF) competition to supply fifth-generation fighters for the United States Air Force, Navy and Marine Corps. Several overseas nations expressed an interest in ordering, or taking part in the programme.

Britain signed up in 2001 as a 'Level 1' major industrial JSF partner, with BAE Systems, Rolls-Royce and others involved in production and support. Britain ordered the F-35B to replace the Panavia Tornado and to return to the carrier-borne strike capability, which had been forsaken with the retirement of the BAe/McDD Harrier force in 2010.

There are three versions: land-based, the 'big-wing' carrier-borne version for the US Navy, and the F-35B for the UK and the US Marines. The F-35B is a STOVL aircraft – short take-off and vertical landing – and is designed to operate from smaller carriers, without the need for catapult launch.

The Lightning II represents a huge leap in capability for the RAF. It will operate alongside the equally potent Eurofighter Typhoon, well into the 2040s if not beyond. The RAF website describes its role as: "a multi-role machine capable of conducting missions including air-to-surface, electronic warfare, intelligence gathering and air-to-air simultaneously.

"F-35B combines advanced sensors and mission systems with low observable technology, or 'stealth', which enables it to operate undetected in hostile airspace. Its integrated sensors, sensor fusion and data linking provide the pilot with unprecedented situational awareness. The pilot is able to share information gathered by the jet with other platforms using secure data links, and/or use the information to employ weapons or electronic countermeasures."

The F-35 is named after the famous twin-engined, twin-boomed, Lockheed P-38 Lightning long-range fighter. The RAF ordered that type in 1940, but initial flight trials in the USA and then at Boscombe Down were highly critical of its performance and it was not adopted. The version issued to Britain lacked turbo-superchargers; P-38s so equipped gave exceptional service with the USAAF.

The RAF does not need to allude

"F-35B combines advanced sensors and mission systems with low observable technology, or 'stealth', which enables it to operate undetected in hostile airspace."

## LOCKHEED MARTIN LIGHTNING II

| | |
|---|---|
| **Type:** | Single-seat STOVL multi-role strike aircraft |
| **First flight:** | December 15, 2006, due to enter service with 617 Squadron in |
| **Powerplant:** | One 40,000lb st (177.88kN) Pratt & Whitey F135 angle-thrust turbofan |
| **Dimensions:** | Span 35ft 0in (10.7m), Length 51ft 2in (15.6m) |
| **Weights:** | All-up approx 60,000lb (27,216kg) |
| **Max speed:** | Quoted as Mach 1.6 |
| **Range:** | 900 miles (1,666km) |
| **Armament:** | Two air-to-air missiles and two 1,000lb (453kg) bombs in weapons bay. Optional 25mm cannon pod. Under wing pylons for up to 15,000lb (6,800kg) of ordinance |
| **Replaces:** | Panavia Tornado GR4 from 2018 |
| **Taken on charge:** | 48 committed against a requirement of 138 |

Marham has been undergoing a massive £500 million transformation since 2016, ready for its new role.

In a similar manner to Joint Force Harrier, the Lightning II fleet will be a combined RAF and Royal Navy operation, staffed with a ratio of 58% and 42% respectively. Trials on board the new aircraft carrier HMS *Queen Elizabeth* are due to commence in late 2018 and from the second vessel, HMS *Prince of Wales*, the following

to its unfortunate experience with the P-38 by sticking to the name Lightning II  it commemorates a home-spun fighter. Between 1970 and 1993 the awesome English Electric Lightning fighter dominated British skies – details in our sister publication *RAF Centenary Celebration Fighters*.

## JOINT FORCE
The RAF has had an F-35B unit since 2014 when 17 Squadron stood up at Edwards Air Force Base, California. The personnel have been evaluating the Lightning II,

developing procedures and tactics ready for its operational debut.

Also in the USA are pilots and technicians who will form the caucus of 617 Squadron at Marham later this year. Based at Beaufort Marine Corps Air Station in South Carolina, these 'pathfinders' have been training alongside the Marines F-35B conversion squadron, VMFAT-501.

Acting as the British operational conversion unit will be 207 Squadron, which will re-form at Marham on July 1, 2019. As the home of the RAF's Tornado force,

year. The first Fleet Air Arm F-35B unit, 809 Squadron, is expected to stand up in 2023.

In its centenary year, the RAF has the heritage, the equipment and the skills to meet its commitments: Agile, Adaptable, Capable. ◉

A pair of the RAF's latest aircraft, Lockheed Martin F-35B Lightning IIs, on exercise in the USA. The first examples for 617 Squadron are due to be delivered to Marham during this centenary year. Since April 2016 the Norfolk base has been undergoing a major refit, estimated to have cost £500 million, to take the new jets. Nuff said. CROWN COPYRIGHT